The Labrador Retriever Training Handbook

———— ❧❧❧❧ ————

The Essential Guide For Potty Training Your Puppy, Teaching Commands, Dog Socialization, And Curbing Bad Behavior

Kimberly Lawrence

Copyright 2018 © Kimberly Lawrence

Legal & Disclaimer

electronically or in print. This extends to creating a secondary or tertiary copy of the work or a recorded copy and is only allowed with an express written consent from the Publisher. All additional right reserved.

The information in the following pages is broadly considered to be a truthful and accurate account of facts, and as such any inattention, use or misuse of the information in question by the reader will render any resulting actions solely under their purview. There are no scenarios in which the publisher or the original author of this work can be in any fashion deemed liable for any hardship or damages that may befall them after undertaking information described herein.

Additionally, the information in the following pages is intended only for informational purposes and should thus be thought of as universal. As befitting its nature, it is presented without assurance regarding its prolonged validity or interim quality. Trademarks that are mentioned are done without written consent and can in no way be considered an endorsement from the trademark holder.

Table of Contents

Introduction

Dogs are man's best friend. For thousands of years, dogs have acted as a companion, a team member, and a comforting friend to people all over the planet. Having a dog in your life can be the difference between a home that is empty, quiet, and lonely and having a home that is vibrant, warm, and loving. Dogs serve as a faithful companion that is always loving and accepting, no matter who you are or what you do.

It is widely believed that dogs were the first animals humans domesticated, going all the way back to the hunter-gatherer days where wolves and humans worked together to find and catch food. Wolves, with their spectacular sense of smell and hearing, would lead humans to the animals they would consider to be prey. Wolves were very good at finding these types of prey animals, but not so good at taking them down. This is where humans, with primitive tools such as bows and arrows and spears, would step in to make the kill. This relationship appeared out of necessity and probably took place independently across hundreds of different groups of people across the world. It isn't known when exactly this practice began, but it likely continued for thousands of years until dogs developed a great trust in humans. Simply put, the dogs more inclined to trust and live in close proximity to humans had a better chance at surviving than the dogs that treated humans with suspicion or hostility.

It is widely known that dogs evolved from some kind of wolf, though all species of wolves that we know today (gray wolves, Indian wolfs) appear to be close enough genetic relatives of the dog to be the species they evolved from. As a result, most researchers believe that the species dogs evolved from is now extinct.

Somewhere along the way during this primitive relationship, humans invented agriculture and more and more of them began to live their lives in one place. As this happened, dogs went from friends on the trail to friends in the home. They became more and more widespread and integrated into the home-centered lifestyle. Somewhere along the line, humans figured out the process of selective breeding and began choosing which dogs to breed together to bring out certain traits that they desired. Over centuries, this led us to develop thousands of different breeds of dogs we see today.

But this book isn't just about any dog. This book is about a breed of dog of which few other types of breeds are more popular, beloved, or instantly recognizable. I am speaking of course about the

Labrador Retriever. Labrador Retrievers are a type of retriever gun-dog. Retrievers are the type of dogs that help hunters by retrieving the prey they kill. Gun-dogs are types of dogs that help hunters both find and retrieve prey, which usually comes in the form of birds or other small game. Labrador Retrievers are very desirable dogs for almost any dog owner. They're friendly, adaptable to most types of lifestyles, and intelligent.

Of course, developing a good relationship with your Labrador Retriever can require more than giving it a home with plenty of space, exercise, and food. Having a well-trained dog has many advantages for both you and your pup.

The first reason having a well-trained dog can improve both you and your dog's life is that the basic nature of the process of training will give the two of you a great bond. Part of the requirements of training is that you and your dog must spend a great amount of time together. This has a few obvious benefits. First, it gives you the chance to really get to know your dog, what they like, what they don't like, and things that may trigger undesirable behavior. Second, it gives your dog a chance to really feel important and valued because of the fact that the two of you are spending so much time together.

The second reason that the process of training your dog can have a positive effect on both of you is the fact that it will inevitably strengthen the bond between both of you. At the same time, as your pup will have an easier time sensing and reacting to your mood, you will also have an easier time sensing and reacting to your pup's mood and actions.

The third benefit of training your Labrador Retriever is that it's fun. Just playing with your dog might get boring at a point, but the process of training is different. As you put in the time to train your dog, you will have the enormous pleasure of watching the fruits of your efforts. As your dog learns to execute the basic commands we'll cover in this text, you get to watch your dog go from a scatter-brained little pup to a full-grown, disciplined dog that gives off distinct vibes of intelligence and understanding.

The next benefit of training your Labrador Retriever is that the process of training often makes undesirable behavior disappear completely from your dog. Most people know someone or have experienced themselves the embarrassment of having an untrained dog displaying just how untrained it is when meeting someone new, either by jumping on them, barking or through some other undesirable behavior. By training, you substantially eliminate the chances of your dog being viewed as undisciplined. It also makes things easier for you in the long run, letting you exercise more control over your dog by expending far less effort.

The next benefit is that the process of training has numerous and enormous benefits for your pup. Learning how to respond to and execute commands gives your dog a sense of purpose in their lives. It makes them feel valued and fulfilled. At the same time, it stimulates your dog's mind and serves as a platform for mental development.

The next benefit is that it improves your dog's life. Dogs that are well-trained are far less likely to be given up or returned to the shelter. They're also far less likely to have to be put down to behavioral issues. Also, the process of training can turn anti-social, shy, or generally fearful dogs into dogs with a healthy amount of confidence and friendliness.

In this book, we're going to cover a lot of topics. We'll discuss what you should know about Labrador Retrievers before you commit as well as things you can do to prepare your home for your new friend. Then we'll go into the different places you can get a Labrador Retriever. I'll give you some suggestions on what to do before you start training as well as the right ages to start prepping your dog for training. Most of the book will be spent describing the different types of strategies for teaching your Labrador Retriever to do basic commands, potty-training, fetching, and how to behave on a leash. We'll also discuss how to understand and learn from your dog's behavior.

What to Know Before You Commit to a Labrador Retriever

C hoosing to get a dog is a potentially decades-long commitment. Like any long-term commitment, you should first make sure you have the resources you need in order to give your new friend a good, loving home. This section will cover everything you need to know in order to set yourself up for a successful relationship with your dog.

What Is a Labrador Retriever?

Labradors are one of the most popular breeds of dogs. They are often trained to be disability assistance dogs for people who are blind, autistic, or have other physical disabilities. They're also often trained to be therapy dogs.

Labrador Retrievers are descendants of the Saint John's Water Dog, which were mainly in England and Newfoundland, Canada. Their ancestors date back to the mid-eighteen hundreds and were a distinct breed of dogs by the 1870s. Their name comes from two places. First, the name "retriever" was given to them because they were often used as hunting dogs and retrieved birds and other small game.

Second, the name "Labrador" comes from the place where they first originated; the Labrador Sea, which lies between the Labrador Peninsula and Greenland off the east coast of Newfoundland.

Labrador Retrievers has a distinct appearance. Their heads are wide with a flat stop at their nose. Their coat is short and dense and has a color dependent on their sub-breed; either yellow, black, or brown. Their body typically is a stout build and is fairly muscular. The Labrador Retriever's size can vary based on whether it is a male or female. Males usually weigh between 65 to 80 pounds while females usually weigh between 55 to 70 pounds.

One thing that sets Labrador Retrievers apart is their temperament. Most Labrador Retrievers are friendly, out-going, and pleasant. They're much less prone to aggression than other dogs of their size, which makes them very good family dogs. This also makes them good for households with other animals which can be either bigger or smaller than themselves. They're also very good around children as it is not easy to make them act aggressively, given that it has been raised in a healthy environment. Labrador Retrievers may bark occasionally, but most of the time they're not overly-noisy, making them very suitable for urban or suburban environments. They're also not usually very territorial, making them excellent pets when in the proximity of other dogs.

Another thing that sets Labrador Retrievers apart from other dogs is their intelligence. This, combined with their friendliness and calm nature, making them very suitable for positions as working dogs. They are used for a variety of purposes. As previously stated, they're often used as disability assistance dogs. But they're also used for a variety of other purposes. They're often used by bird-hunters to retrieve game. They're also capable of emergency assistance in people prone to seizures and other fits of unconsciousness.

The Types of Labrador Retrievers

There are two main, distinct types of Labrador Retrievers: Yellow Labrador Retrievers and Chocolate Labrador Retrievers. They came about through a few dog breeders who wanted a type of dog that was cool-headed and would bring the game back unharmed to hunters. Today, most Labrador Retrievers live out their lives as simple pets for families.

The Yellow Labrador Retrievers we know today, like almost all dogs, were much different than the dogs they descended from. Back in the mid-nineteenth century, the "yellow" Labrador Retrievers were still yellow but were a much darker shade than the ones we know today. In fact, their coats were what we would call butterscotch, much darker than what we know today. For a while, these types of dogs were called Golden Retrievers, but this was changed by the UK Kennel Club on the grounds that "golden" was not a color. This type of Labrador Retriever went through a slow but consistent change in their appearance over the course of the 20th century as it was common for people to desire lighter-colored yellow dogs over the dirty-looking yellow dogs. As a result, more and more breeders centered on making their pups more cream colored in order to sell more dogs. Over the course of decades, this practice gave way to the light-colored Yellow Golden Retrievers we know today.

Chocolate Labs were not considered a distinct breed until about half-way through the 20th century. While some researches have traced modern Chocolate Labrador Retrievers to a few original bloodlines, some believe their appearance to be the result of cross-breeding, specifically with the Flat-Coated Retriever as well as the Chesapeake Bay Retriever. This was mostly done during the 20th century in Newfoundland. By the second half of the 20th century, Chocolate Labrador Retrievers were known as a distinct breed in the kennels of the Earl of Feversham.

Besides dividing the types of Labrador Retrievers by their color types, there's also a division to be made by origin as well as purpose. These two types are the English Labrador and the American Labrador. The English Labrador is more often used for dog shows and other such types of competitions. The American Labrador is more often used as a working dog and as a family pet.

The American Labrador is usually sharper and more physically fit than its English counterpart. It's also largely more reactive than English Labradors. This isn't to say that they are more prone to bad behavior, just that they're more sensitive to their surroundings. As a whole, they still have a good temperament compared to other dog breeds. They also have more energy than English Labradors. This is because they're more often been bred as working dogs as well as hunting dogs. This means that your Labrador Retriever will require a good amount of activity and exercise to keep it happy.

English Labrador Retrievers often weigh more than their American Labrador Retriever counterparts. They also typically have shorter, stouter arms and legs. While they are active with a lot of energy when they are young dogs, most American Labrador Retrievers grow into more active adult dogs than English Labrador Retrievers who tend to become calmer and less active when they get older. As puppies, they're also often harder to train than American Labrador Retrievers because they are more scatterbrained on average. They like to play and might get distracted more easily.

There are subtle differences between the different types of Labrador Retrievers, but these differences shouldn't necessarily dissuade you from getting a certain one. They are, as a breed, largely friendly, easy to control, and wonderful companions.

Is a Labrador Retriever Right for You?

There are several things to consider before you commit to a Labrador Retriever. One concern many people have when considering getting a large dog as active as a Labrador Retriever is whether or not they have enough space to keep their dog happy, though this isn't as big of a concern as you might think. Having a huge amount of space for your Labrador Retriever to stomp around on doesn't mean much if you aren't consistently spending time with it. They're not going to be active (or happy) if they're left alone by themselves day after day. What's really important to consider is whether you have enough time to spend with it during the day. Just going for an hour long walk every day is probably sufficient to keep your Labrador Retriever healthy and happy.

Another thing to consider is whether or not your home itself is big enough to keep a Labrador Retriever happy. For example, if you're living in a small apartment and will be gone for a majority of the day, you shouldn't get a dog that requires the kind of space and activity that a Labrador Retriever does. They also like to be involved in things. If you're looking for a dog that likes to sit on the couch and watch you go about your day, a Labrador Retriever isn't for you. They like to play and be involved in most of what they see going on.

Another thing to consider before getting a Labrador Retriever is whether or not you have the funds to take proper care of a Labrador Retriever. The costs can be more expensive than you might think. Expenses like vaccinations are obvious medical costs, but should your dog get sick or get injured in some way, vet bills can get into the thousands. If you have a dog that's in an environment that might make it prone to injury (like a rural area with wild animals or farm animals). This is a possibility that happens to many pet owners. A smart thing you can do to prepare yourself for this by protecting yourself financially and making sure your pet can get the care it needs is to get pet insurance. This is usually paid monthly and can stack up over time, but it is worth it to have a plan to pay for vet expenses should your dog have some medical issue that requires expensive operations. Labradors also have many diseases they can inherit.

Besides vet expenses, there's also the cost of food and grooming tools to think about. You also might want to consider the costs of getting a chip put in your dog should they get lost. That way, you'll have a way of easily finding them.

Another thing you should consider before getting a Labrador Retriever is the amount of clean-up you'll have to do for your dog. Unlike us, dogs do not have the desire to keep themselves or their environments clean. They like to roll around in the mud and get dirty. They have no problem getting wet. If your dog is going to be going outside and inside a lot, it's inevitable they're going to get dirty at least a few times. This can mean them tracking mud into your house as well as stinking up the place with that "wet-dog smell." If you're very afraid of germs and can't stand getting your hands or your house dirty (even if it can be easily cleaned up), you might want to consider that before getting a Labrador Retriever.

Why Are Labrador Retrievers so Popular?

The Labrador Retrievers are the most popular dog breeds in the United States, and there are many reasons for that.

First, Labrador Retrievers are highly intelligent. There's a reason they are so often used as service dogs. They are fast learners and quick to pick up on new commands. Not only does this make them easy to control, but it also makes them very compatible with jobs and tasks many other dogs couldn't do. They like challenges and doing new things, making them good pets for people that are adventurous and would like to have a dog that's easily handled.

Labrador Retrievers are also popular because they are very gentle dogs who are not prone to aggression. Certain breeds of dogs are very territorial or defensive of their home turf or food (there's actually a test to measure how aggressive a dog is by sticking a fake hand into a food dish while the dog is eating). These types of problems are not often found in Labrador Retrievers. This means that they are a good choice for people in environments that are more social or chaotic than usual, as Labrador Retrievers are good at adapting non-aggressively to these types of environments. As a result, Labrador Retrievers are a good choice for people who have households with other dogs or small children. Labrador Retrievers are actually well-known for the gentleness they show when they're around children. Like all puppies, Labradors can bite and nip from time to time when they're young. But this habit is much easier to train out of them than it is in most other dog breeds. They can learn how to be gentle without sacrificing the joy you'll get with playing with them. Besides getting along very easily with other dogs, Labs love company in the form of all kinds of animals including cats, goats, ferrets, and any other type of furry pet you might have in or around your home.

While Labrador Retrievers do have certain inherited diseases they are at risk for (which is true for almost every type of dog breed), they have, on average, fewer health problems than other breeds of dogs. This gives a number of different benefits for the owner.

First, it relieves the stress that comes with owning a dog that has habitual health problems. Second, it means the owners of Labrador Retrievers will not have the same kind of financial strain due to vet expenses that some other owners of different breeds of dogs often face. Third, it means that your Labrador Retriever will be a part of your family for a long time. Labradors live long, active lives; still loving exercise, games, and activity well past when they turn a decade old.

Another benefit of owning a Labrador Retriever is the fact that they're easier to groom than other breeds that shed more often or have longer, thicker, and messier coats. This saves you trips to the groomer as well as the dreaded dog hair all around your house and furniture.

Labrador Retrievers also are good helpers. They love to be involved and are always excited to have "jobs" or certain purposes they can help you with. They love to tag along while playing sports and are quite competitive with other dogs when playing their own games. You'll never have a problem getting your Lab off the couch.

Labs also have very versatile diets. They don't need high-end pet food (though it helps) to stay healthy, active, and full of energy. Dogs can eat almost anything, and Labs are no exception. Another aspect of Labs that people might not immediately think as being a benefit is that there is plenty of them available. Being the most popular dog breed in the United States means that it's a pretty safe bet that you can find breeders of Labs in your area as well as at almost any pound or human society.

Getting a Labrador Retriever

There are many easy ways to get a Labrador Retriever. Based on how much you're willing to spend, what age of Lab you want, and whether having a pure-bred Labrador Retriever matters to you, there are certain things you should know about the different places to adopt or buy a Labrador Retriever before you make the commitment. In this section, we'll cover some of the most common places people find their new best friends.

Types of Dog Breeders

Not all dog breeders are created equal. While most of them can offer the same thing (pure-bred dogs or desirable mixes), knowing what to look for in the different places that breed dogs is important for two main reasons. First, it can mean the difference between getting a healthy dog and a sick dog. Second, it can stop you from supporting cruel businesses that breed their dogs in inhumane ways such as "puppy mills." These places raise dogs, cats, and other domesticated animals in environments that are often dirty, unsanitary, crowded, cruel, and generally do not provide a good place for these animals to live.

If you're looking to get a dog from a breeder, you should know how to find and identify what is called a *Responsible Breeder*. Before we discuss what makes a responsible breeder, we'll start by discussing the places you should always avoid. You are probably familiar with at least a few types of retail chain pet-stores such as Petco, PetSmart, Petland, Pet Supplies Plus, and many other retail chain pet-stores. While we can't say that every animal these stores sell come from puppy mills or other such places, we can safely say that they have been known to get their animals from breeders that would be considered puppy mills. At any one of these locations, you can't know what kind of environment these animals come from. By buying animals from these places, you are inadvertently supporting these kinds of inhumane breeders.

Now we'll talk about how to find a Responsible Breeder. Breeders can range from a small operation done only part-time, to a huge farm that has hundreds of different dogs. But no matter what the size, there are a few things you can do to ensure that you're getting your dog from a humane place.

First, you should the breeder is knowledgeable about the dogs they're raising and kind to them. Second, you should ask to visit the environment where the dogs are raised in and also to see the parents of the dog you're interested in buying. This can give you an idea of what the dog's behavior will be when they are grown. Third, you should take a good, long look at the kennels or general property. You should look to make sure the area is clean, that the dogs have plenty of space and food, and for any signs of bad health such as sores, patches of bare skin, and other such signs. Lastly, make sure the breeders are open and honest about any problems they've encountered with their dogs. They should not seem secretive or put off by questions you have every right to ask.

One benefit of getting you Lab from breeders is that you can usually get them as puppies, making them easier to train and more easily integrated into your home. By buying from breeders, you have the opportunity to see both the parents of the dogs as well as the environment in which they were raised. It is also easier to get Labs that are purely labs, or at least Labs for which you know exactly what it is mixed with if it is a mix.

A few disadvantages of getting your Lab from breeders is that it can sometimes be hard to find a good breeder if you live in a sparsely populated area. They are also probably the most expensive place to get your Lab compared to pounds or humane societies, which we will talk about next.

Shelters, Rescues, and Pounds

Shelters, rescues, and pounds are often used interchangeably, but they are quite different from each other. A majority of the dogs that end up in these places aren't there because they're bad dogs or did anything wrong. Usually, dogs end up in these places because their previous owners had to give them up due to circumstances outside of their control. So don't be scared. All of these places are filled with friendly dogs that will make wonderful pets!

Rescues accept dogs that shelter or pound either couldn't or wouldn't take. This can be because of a few reasons. First, shelters and pounds, especially in large cities, are prone to overcrowding and often simply don't have space for some certain unfortunate dogs. They also might not take dogs because of aggressive or other types of undesirable behavior, usually stemming from abuse. Rescues, which are usually non-profit organizations operated by volunteers, take these dogs in and often focus on rehabilitation and placement. One benefit of getting a dog from rescues is that the staff there will usually have a good idea of the dog's needs, temperament, and other personality traits which can help you decide whether or not the dog is a good fit for your home.

Probably the best-known animal shelter in the United States is the Humane Society. They are privately owned charities. Shelters can be as small as having a few dogs looking for a home to as big as having hundreds of dogs on its property. Some are even as big as to have full on marketing teams that hold events for adoption or for fundraising. Like rescues, these organizations can give you a good idea of the behavior of any certain dog before you take it home. But they can be pretty busy, so it may be up to you to follow up on a potential pet. Shelters, unlike rescues, which almost never euthanize animals, could be 'kill shelters' or 'no-kill shelters'. Kill shelters usually keep the dog for a while if they think it's a good candidate for adoption. But, depending on the amount of space available and the number of dogs coming in, they might end up having to put certain dogs down. So if you get your dog from a shelter, you might be saving a life.

Pounds are the saddest type of place you can get a dog from. Unlike shelters or rescues, they don't have much of a focus on saving the lives of animals. The dogs in pounds are usually strays who have been found or pets who have been given up by their owner. If the dog is a stray, the pound gives them a certain amount of time for their owner to claim them, as is required by law. If their owner doesn't show up to claim them, they can be given a little more time to for someone else to come in to adopt them, either a private citizen or a rescue group. If this doesn't happen quickly enough, the dog is usually put down. If you get a dog from a pound, there's a good chance you're saving its life. Unfortunately, the staff there probably doesn't have the resources to really assess the dog, so it's hard to know what kind of dog you're getting.

Starting Young

Once you've found your new Labrador Retriever, there are some things you should know before you bring it home. And, once you've brought it home, if you wish to train it, there are some things you can do right off the bat to give your dog a head start on its training. In this section, we'll cover how to prepare your home for your new Lab. We'll also talk about what to expect during the first week as well as some simple things you can do to prepare it for training as well as what you should do to directly prepare it for training. Then we'll go over how to start curbing basic behavior. Finally, we'll go over how to teach your dog some basic commands every dog should know.

Preparing Your Home

If you're living with other people, the first thing you should make sure of before you bring a dog into your home is that they are okay and ready to share their home with a new friend. This ensures a smooth transition for yourself as you open your home to a dog. It also makes sure that your dog is given a warm, loving environment when it arrives at your home. Everyone in the home should know the breed of the dog, the age of the dog, and perhaps even an idea of its temperament.

Next, you should get everyone in your home on the same page as to which behaviors you either want or don't want in your dog. Everyone should be consistent in which behaviors the dog should be dissuaded from. For example, if you want to stop your dog from excessive licking or biting, everyone in the home should know that this behavior is not acceptable and they should also know the way you're going to curb the behavior. With everyone in the house reacting the same way to a dog's certain behavior, it will make it much easier and quicker to break the dog of that behavior.

Next, you should make sure you have dished for food and water ready at home. You should also have a kind of dog food that is made specifically for your dog's size, age, and activity level. Next, if you're planning on training your dog, you should have treats ready to go so you can start training immediately. This can be dog biscuits, a piece of lunch meat, cheese, or any other type of treat your dog loves to eat. You should also have a collar and leash ready as well as any other type of dog-related tool you might need.

Next, you should set aside certain areas for your dog. If you don't want your Lab on the couch, make sure they have a comfortable, warm place to sleep and relax instead. This can be in the form of a dog bed or simply in the form of a few old blankets, pillows, or quilts.

You should also make sure that your dog has a place to exercise and go to the bathroom. If you have a backyard, you have three options. If your yard has a fence that your lab won't be able to get out of, you can plan on just letting them roam around the backyard. If your fence needs repairs or fixing, make sure that is done before you bring your Lab home. If you don't have a way to keep your dog in or don't want it roaming freely around your yard for whatever reason, you should have a way to tether it to a certain area, either with a rope or a small chain. Or, if you live in a rural area far enough away from busy roads or neighbors, you can plan on just letting your dog run free around your home. They'll know your house is their home in a very short amount of time, though if they start to roam, you might want to restrict their movement.

If you have a puppy, you'll want to make sure your home is "puppy-proof" by putting things that can be chewed up away or out of reach. Puppies have new teeth coming in. As a result, they live to bite and chew on things. Some of the things you should put away or out of reach are shoes, TV remotes, clothes, socks, paper, stuffed animals, and anything else a puppy could chew on. You can also use a type of spray to coat the legs of furniture and other such things that can't be moved to deter your Lab pup from chewing on them. These types of sprays make the surfaces taste bad and unpleasant to your pup. One thing you definitely want to get your Lab pup is something they can chew on because they need to chew on something. This can be a rope, a bone, or some kind of chew-toy.

The First Week

The first week your dog is home will set the mood and dynamic for your whole relationship.

The first thing you should do is give your Lab pup a name. You should use it as often as you can. Chances are they won't respond right away. Something you can do to speed this process up is to call them by their name and then give them a treat. This will make them associate the sound of their name with the pleasure of getting the treat. If you repeat this enough, every time you say their name, you'll get their immediate attention.

One thing you should do is restrict your pup's movement, keeping it in your line of sight when possible. If you get a Lab puppy, it's unavoidable that they're going to get into some sort of trouble, either chewing something up, knocking stuff over, or going to the bathroom where they shouldn't. You should, if possible, keep your pup out of rooms with carpet, making clean-up easy should they have an accident. This also keeps them from getting into certain rooms that have things they can damage. You can do this by blocking off certain stairways or hallways or by simply shutting a door.

You also want to get your pup on a routine. It might sound strange, but putting some order into a Lab pup's life can make them better behaved, calmer, and more easily trained. Your Lab pup should wake up and go to bed at the same time every day. It helps them get used to the home and the people in it. You should also try to feed and water them at the same time every day. This will help them regulated their digestive system and will reduce the number of accidents.

You should also give them potty breaks as often as possible. If you're home, try to take them out about once an hour, keeping an eye on them and letting them back in directly after they go to the bathroom. This will make them associate the outside with going to the bathroom much quicker than they would otherwise.

During the first week, you want to keep the vibe calm in the house. Moving homes is a big deal to a Lab pup, and it can cause a certain amount of stress. Of course, everyone in the house will want to see and play with the pup. This is okay, but remember that your Lab pup is still growing and developing, and needs a lot of rest as a result. Make sure your home is as free as it can be from loud noises or general chaos for the first couple weeks your Lab pup is home. Don't push them into doing things they're not comfortable with. As your Lab pup gets more comfortable with its environment, it will explore on its own. This isn't to say that you shouldn't play with your new lab pup. You absolutely should. It keeps them active and serves as a great way to bond with them. It also ensures that they'll be tired when it's time to go to bed. Just to be sure not to be too intense when playing with them.

Another thing you should do during the first week your Lab pup is home is to make sure they have a place to sleep that they are comfortable with. When everything gets dark and quiet in this new, unfamiliar place they find themselves in, chances are they're going to get a little scared. This means they might whine and wake you up during the night. Some things you should do to help them feel more comfortable is to make sure they have a place to sleep that is their own. You may also want to make sure they're not sleeping alone. You can put their bed into your bedroom during the first week to make them feel more comfortable with sleeping by knowing they're close to you.

Preparing Your Labrador Retriever Puppy for Training

Puppies have notoriously short attention spans. It also takes Lab pups a while to get used to and comfortable with their environment. Because of these things, it's not a smart idea to start obedience training right away. Not only will they probably not be receptive to it, but it can also give them the wrong idea of you being too demanding or controlling. It used to be the rule that you shouldn't start obedience training until they're six months old. It still is, to an extent, and we'll talk more about that later. Still, there are some basic games you can play to prepare them to respond to commands while still being fun for them.

A basic game you can do with your Lab puppy requires a few people. At least three people are needed, but it gets really fun once you have five or six. Once you have enough people, give them all a few dog treats and have them all stand or sit in a type of circle with lots of space in between them. Put the Lab pup in the middle of the group and take turns calling its name. When it comes to you when you call its name, give it a treat. This game can help them be responsive and attentive while also making them like everyone a lot more.

Another thing you can do requires at least two people. One person gets the puppies attention while the other person gently holds it in the place. Then the first person goes out of sight and hides somewhere, either inside the house or outside the house. Keep calling the lab pup's name, and reward it with a treat and praise when it finds you. As you guys keep playing this game, you can go further and further away. This game teaches your dog to respond to its name while also giving them the challenge of finding you.

A simple game you can do with your puppy requires just yourself, a leash, some treats, and a place to explore. Go somewhere outside where the Lab pup hasn't been before. Let them stop and go where they want, letting them stop to smell or look around. As the Lab pup does this, they'll occasionally look back at you. So every time they look back at you, praise them and give them a treat. Do this over and over again for a while until they're looking back at you constantly. If they don't look at you right away, say their name and give them a treat when they look back. This prepares them for future leash training and makes them more in tune to yourself.

The last basic game you can play with your dog to prepare it for training is the old game of tug of war. It keeps them active and healthy and will wear them out in a pretty short time, making them quieter when it's time to go to bed later. This game can be used to teach your pup two things; when to pick up the toy and when to let the rope go. Choose a different command for both actions and reward them with a treat when they complete the command.

Basic Training

While it may be a while before you should start teaching your dog basic obedience training such as sitting, laying down, staying, or coming, you can almost immediately start trying to control your Lab pup's behavior. Most of this section will be about the different ways you can curb bad behavior in general (we'll get into how to curb specific bad behaviors later in the book).

One thing we should establish right away is that

you should try to train your lab pup without using punishment. While physically reprimanding your dog has the reputation of teaching it that you are the dominant one in the group, today it is widely known that this isn't the best way to curb unwanted behaviors. Physically punishing your dog make them more prone to aggressive behavior because you are yourself displaying aggression and dogs largely pick up their behavior and temperament from their owners. It can turn a Lab pup with a few bad behaviors into a dog that's hostile and prone to biting.

Another thing you shouldn't do when trying to curb your Lab pup's bad behavior is to act aggressively towards it. This includes holding it down, staring at it intensely, and intimidating you Lab pup. Using these kinds of methods may curb bad behavior, but it also teaches your dog to act aggressively in certain situations. And that is something you don't ever want in a dog, especially if it's around small children or other animals.

You also shouldn't raise your voice at your Lab pup. When young dogs get scared, they may bow down to you, but it can lead to resentment that results in aggression in the long run. Young dogs usually pick up their temperament from their owners. So if you're anxious and nervous around them, chances are they're also going to grow up to be anxious and nervous. In the exact same way, if you are loud and angry towards your lab pup, chances are they're going to end up being a loud and angry dog.

Now that we've covered the things you shouldn't do when trying to control your Lad pup's behavior, let's go over what you should to curb your lab pup's behavior. The first thing you can do to accomplish this is very simple: be consistent. If you allow or even reward a bad behavior even once, your Lab pup will have in its mind that it's okay in some sense, even if you discourage it a majority of the time. Switching between allowing a bad behavior and discouraging a bad behavior can also confuse your Lab pup, causing stress and perhaps even resentment.

Also, make sure to only discipline your Lab pup if you can catch them while doing the unwanted behavior. If you discipline your pup for something it did a few hours ago, it's not gonna connect the dots between what it did and what it is being disciplined for, even if you try to show them what they did wrong. Even a span of a few minutes between the bad behavior and the discipline can confuse your Lab pup.

While you never want to yell at or physically punish your dog, that doesn't mean you shouldn't take a hard stand against unwanted behavior. You shouldn't raise your voice, but consistently giving them a strong "no" when they do something wrong accompanied by being put outside or a timeout will make them associate that sound with something they shouldn't do which makes it much easier to curb bad behavior in you Lab pup.

Something you can do that will enforce positive behavior while also winning over your Lab pup's affection is using positive reinforcement. It's important to discipline your pup when they display some kind of bad, unwanted behavior. But, at the same time, it's also important to reward them for positive behavior. You can reward them with praise, with pets, or with their favorite kind of treat.

A good way you can discipline any young Lab pup is through giving them timeouts. While it isn't as harsh as punishing them physically or yelling at them, placing them into isolation directly after they do something bad can be a great way to curb unwanted behavior. In the same way that little kids get bored during timeouts and hate them, dogs are also not big fans of timeouts. They like to play and lock their attention to something. So timeouts can be a great way of curbing behavior by putting them through something they don't like while not confusing, upsetting, or triggering aggression in them. When you put your dog in timeout, you should have prepared some specific verbal signal that is distinct from all other commands.

Without acting angry or upset, you can then gently lead them to a room or area that's small and has little to no things that can entertain your Lab pup. Separating your dog from other dogs or people is a mildly unpleasant experience, and, if you are consistent in meeting bad behaviors with this discipline tactic, it won't take long for them to associate that behavior with something that is unpleasant. This shouldn't be for too long a period of time. Also, they should have access to food and water to keep them comfortable. If they get hungry or thirsty and don't have access to food or water, it can cause them to panic as well as build resentment towards whoever is depriving them of these things.

Essential Commands

There is no magic age at which you should start training your dog. Every dog is different. If you've been preparing them for training by playing certain games and curbing bad behavior, you can probably start training around four to five months old. If you've been waiting until your dog matures to train them, then six to seven months old are probably a good suggestion as to when to start. Whatever age your dog is, you should make sure they can focus and pay attention to you for a good amount of time, as you can't train a dog to do much when they're not even looking or listening to you. If needed, you can go back to some of the games for puppies we've already described to help train your dog to pay attention to you.

Some of the things you should make sure of before beginning to train your dog these basic commands are that you have plenty of time, are well rested and are in a good mood. Some dogs pick up on training quicker than other dogs, but it's safe to say that training any dog requires a lot of patience. You don't want to get frustrated with your dog while training because they can sense your mood, and being afraid of you while learning these commands will cause them stress both during the process as well as every time you give them the command in the future.

In this section, we'll go over some easy ways to train your Labrador Retriever to do the basic commands. As we've already discussed, Labrador Retrievers are smarter than most other dog breeds, so they'll probably be quicker to pick up on these commands than other dogs would be. That is if they're trained the correct way using the correct methods. The purpose of this section is to teach you how to do that in the most effective way possible.

How to Come

Even if you're not interested in teaching your dog some of the harder commands, one thing all dogs should be able to do is to come to their owner on command. So here's how to do it.

Take your dog and bring them into your home. Make sure you have plenty of their favorite treats. Choose a quiet room that is as free as possible of distractions. Then sit with your dog right next to you and say their name and "come" until they look at you. When they look at you, give them a treat. This is all they have to do at first. Do this many times until they begin to react to only the word "come."

Once they can do this well, put a treat on the floor beneath them. When they're done eating it, say "come" again. When they look at you, give them a treat. Do this over and over again. Slowly, start dropping the treat further and further away from them until they have to walk over and get it, saying "come" when they're furthest from you and rewarding them with a treat when they come to you. Just say the word "come" as much as you can and only use their name if they're really not responding. Using their name too much can make them ignore it after a while. Try to say the command only once. Saying it too often can result in them not responding to it. If they don't come to you when you say the command, take a step closer to them and repeat until they come to you.

Once your puppy learns how to turn around when he hears the command, begin increasing the distance and changing other aspects of the command. Throw the treat further and further. After a while, you can even begin to take a few steps back or move to a different part of the room while they're going after or eating the treat. Once they can respond to your command without fail no matter how far the distance is between you or what part of the room you're in, you can move to other parts of the house and try to call them from other rooms. As you do this, see if they'll come to you without you throwing a treat while still rewarding them with one.

Once they've mastered this, move outside and practice this command over as long a distance as you can. Slowly, start phasing out rewarding them with treats of any kind except praise, rewarding them with treats only if you have to if they start to drop off.

How to Sit

Having a dog that knows how to sit is one of those things most dogs can or should know how to do. While it may not be the most fun, it is a useful command because it keeps your dog in tune with you and reminds them that you are in control.

There are two main ways through which you can teach your dog how to sit.

The first way we'll discuss is called *capturing*. You start by standing before your Labrador Retriever pup while holding some of their favorite treats in your hand. When you start, he should be in the standing position. You should be making eye-contact with him the entire time you're doing this. If you do this for a long enough, they should eventually sit at some point. When you see them do this, praise them and give them a treat. After they've sat down and you've rewarded them, you should now take a step back and keep moving back until they stand up. Once they stand up, keep waiting while holding eye-contact and wait for them to sit and reward them. Repeat the same process, but say sit when they stand up and keep repeating the command until they do it, and then reward them. Do this same process for as long as it takes until they can sit by hearing just one command.

The next method of teaching your dog to sit is called *luring*. This method of training requires a more intimate interaction with your dog. First, make sure you have plenty of treats they like. Then find a room or a place that has as few distractions as possible. What you want to do is hold the treat right in front of your Lab pup's nose without letting them bite at it or lick at it. Once your Lab pup is nice and focused on it, slowly lift it up while making sure they're following the motion of the treat. As you do this, you should make their nose follows the treat and begins to point up high enough. Eventually, your Lab pup should sit down in order to lift their nose up higher. When they sit, give the treat to them and give them praise. Repeat this a few times. Once they've gotten the hang of it, leave the treats behind and just use your hand to guide them up to the position of sitting. Keep doing this a few times the same way. Once they get the hang of it, start saying "sit" as you guide them up with your hand. Make sure you say the word "sit" right before you give them the hand signal. Repeat this over and over again while slowly phasing out the hand signal until they sit just from the command.

How to Lay Down

You can teach your Lab pup to lay down in the same kind of way you can teach them to sit. Move them into a quiet room with as few distractions as possible and make sure you bring plenty of their favorite treats. Then stand or sit before them while being silent and not moving. Eventually, your dog will either sit or lie down. When your Lab pup lies down, praise them and give them a treat and praise while saying "lay down" or whatever it is you want the command to be. Then prompt them to stand back up using "stand up" or some other cue. If they don't want to stand up right away, you can prompt them to by holding a treat out of their reach, making them stand up to get it. Then wait for them to lay down again, giving them a treat, praising them, and saying the command as they do so. Slowly, you can start phasing out using the treat and just use hand signals. Once they can obey the hand signals without fail, slowly phase them out and only use the command.

You can also use the technique of luring to teach them how to law down. Hold one of their favorite treats beneath their nose and move it down as they try to eat it until they lay down on the floor. When they're on the floor, give them the treat and praise them while saying "lay down" or some other command. Repeat this for as long as it takes until they can do it quickly and consistently without fail. Once they can do this, slowly start phasing out using the treat and only use your hand while still praising them and repeating the command. Once they can lay down only using your hand motion, slowly start phasing out the hand motion and only use the command.

How to Stay

Having a dog that knows how to stay can mean the difference between having a dog that is wild and uncontrollable to having a dog that's easy to control and won't be hard to get a hold of should they get away from you in public for whatever reason. While it may seem like a simple command like the others we've covered so far, correctly teaching a dog how to stay is a lot harder than you may think. Basically what you're doing is teaching your dog to ignore its surrounding and all outside stimuli except for yourself. This section will give you a few different ways to teach your Lab pup how to stay successfully.

Teaching a Lab pup how to stay is more than

getting them to sit still on command. In fact, it has two parts. The first is obeying the command you give that signals them to sit. The second is obeying the command you give them that's meant to tell them that they're free to get up. Before you start teaching your dog how to stay, you should've first taught them how to sit. This is necessary for the training process and they should be able to do it consistently.

Really, the words you use for these two commands can be whatever you want. The meaning they have to your dog will depend on what you train them to associate with it. All it is to them is a sound. Knowing this, you should make sure that these two commands sound very distinctly different. This is also true for every other command you might train your dog to respond to. For the command that prompts them to stay, we'll just use "stay" for the purposes of this section. For the command that tells them they can move freely, we'll use "ok" for this section.

In what may seem backward, you should begin by teaching them the command that tells them they can move freely. First, go to a place where there isn't much sound and is free from distractions. Make sure you have plenty of their favorite treats. To start, stand with your Lab pup on one side of the space you're in, making sure they can be held in place. Next, throw one of their treats to the other side of the space you're in. Instead of keeping them from getting the treat, immediately let them go over and get it. As soon as they start over towards it, say the word you've previously chosen that tells them they're free to move. Repeat this process a good number of times, maybe fifteen to twenty at most. This will teach your Lab pup that the sound you're making means to start walking.

Once your dog knows the sound that tells them they're free to move, make sure you're facing them, prompt them to sit, and praise them with a treat and release them with the word you've already decided on. Then prompt them to sit and face them again, waiting about five seconds before you repeat the same process. Then wait and praise them again with another treat when you release them with the specific word. Do this again and again. Start adding five seconds to the time you wait between each treat you give them. What you're doing here is rewarding them for staying still. Somewhere along the way, your Lab pup will probably move or get up before you release them. All this means is that you have to go back five seconds and increase the time interval slower.

Once your dog can sit for a good amount of time, start adding distance between the two of you. Give them the prompt to sit and then give them the prompt that means "stay" before moving away from them. Take just one step away at first. Then repeat the same process as above after a few seconds of waiting while slowly increasing the distance. If your Lab pup moves before you give them the prompt, simply repeat the process over while moving a shorter distance away from them than you did before. You should build the distance between the two of you very slowly. This makes it easier for your dog and decreases stress for both of you. Once you've gone the distance, give the release word and let them come over to you, prompting them with a treat if needed (treats should be phased out eventually, however).

At first, you should be taking steps backward, facing them the entire time. As the distance increases and they get better at following your commands, begin turning your back to them while walking only short distances at first. You should make sure they can stay while watching you move away a good distance before you proceed to the next step. Once they can, start giving them the prompt to stay while standing a little further away than before. Then give them the release prompt and let them come over to you. Once they can obey the "stay" command and the "free to go" command at a good distance, throw a treat a few feet away. Once they get to it, tell them to stay, wait, and them prompt them to walk away or come over to you. Keep increasing the distance you can throw the treat with them still obeying you until they can do it at great distance without fail.

Teaching them how to stay is a big process that can take a few hours. You may even want to split the process up over a few days to keep them from getting tired or stressed.

How to Potty-Train Your Labrador Retriever

T eaching your Labrador Retriever where it can and can't go to the bathroom is something you should start doing as early as possible. One of the most common reasons owners give up dogs is because they make these kinds of messes inside the house. Putting up with a dog who you constantly have to clean up after is a hard thing to do. Unless your dog has been potty-trained before you took it home, there will be accidents. The only thing you can do for these is to prepare. Make sure you have paper towels, anti-septic, gloves, and other cleaning supplies. You should also, if possible, restrict your lab pup's movement to places where they can't leave stains. This means not letting them onto furniture until they're broken-in. It also means putting up barriers around your house to keep you Lab pup out of rooms with carpet floors. If you can, try to restrict their movement to rooms with hardwood floors because these floors are much easier to clean up messes on.

Anyone who has ever had a dog will probably tell you that they know how to break a dog in. One of the most common methods (among Americans at least) of house-training your new Lab pup is to rub their nose in their own urine or feces. In regards to this method, there is one thing I want to make clear: you should never do this. While it may teach your dog now to potty inside of the house in the long run, it's a cruel form of punishment for something they don't know better than to do. Dogs have no instinct that tells them there are places they should go and shouldn't go. Using this method of house-training will only make your dog fear you as well as fearing being inside. This can lead to aggression in certain dogs, ruining your relationship with them.

In this section, I'll cover three different types of ways to house-train your dogs. They all have different purposes and are better suited for different environments. Coming up, I'll define the different types and give you an idea of which types of homes are compatible with which type of house training. Then I'll go through and describe the process of teaching your dog each method.

Finally, I'll end this section with some very helpful tips to speed up or maintain your dog's behavior.

Kinds of Housetraining and the Types of Homes They're Suited For

There are three main methods for house-training your dog: crate training, outside training, and paper training. We'll go over them in that order.

Crate Training

The method of Crate Training can turn some people off. If you have empathy for Labs at all, you'd probably expect to feel guilty at the idea of keeping your new friend locked in a cage inside your home. But dogs love crates! They have an instinctual desire to seek out a small, confined, and comfortable place that they can turn into their own space. Chances are that, whether or not you provide your new pup with a crate, they'll find some sort of small space where they can sleep.

There's also a lot of benefits for dog owners when they decide to crate train their dog. Having a comfortable and safe place you can put your dog into comes in handy if your dog is excitable (which most young dogs are) and you're having company over, especially considering that you don't have to worry about them making a mess. It's also nice for those who live in apartments or those who can't put their dogs outside for some reason. Also, if you ever need to take your dog somewhere, such as to the vet or on a trip, then crate training will make sure your Lab is already comfortable with being in a crate for extended periods of time.

The concept of crate training requires that the crate is large enough that the dog can relieve itself inside it while still keeping the space where they sleep/lounge clean. Like us, dogs don't like laying in their own waste, so having a specific corner sectioned off for their bathroom needs will prompt them to go there every time.

Outside Training

The concept of outside training is simple; your new Lab pup does its business outside. Sounds simple, right? Well, you'd be interested to know that outside training is actually the hardest method of house-training to do. In the process of house-training, you're probably going to see more accidents than any other method.

Training your dog to go to the bathroom can fit your needs for a number of reasons. If you have multiple dogs, it ensures that you won't have to clean up too many messes once you get them broken in. Or, if your dog is big, it can stop you from cleaning up after them too.

The best kind of environment for outside potty-training your pup is a house with a yard that's either fenced in or a home in a rural area far away from roads and other houses. But if you don't have this kind of place, that's fine too. Just make sure you're okay with taking your dog outside on a leash multiple times a day.

Also, just because your dog does its business outside doesn't mean you won't have to clean up the mess. If you live in an apartment complex or in a condo, you probably know that many of these places require you to pick up after your dog. So make sure you have access to gloves and bags!

Paper Training

Paper training got its name from dog-owners in high-rise apartments who, instead of taking their dog down a bunch of floors, simply laid down some newspapers and let their dog do its business on those. Of course, if you want, you can still use newspapers for this purpose, just make sure you put down a bunch of them and be prepared to clean up the floor underneath. For the most part, however, most people using this method opt for special pads that are designed to be absorbent and sanitary.

This method is a good choice for owners who live in high-rise apartments or other heavily urban areas that might make it hard for you to take your dog outside. It's also a good alternative method for Lab-owners that either doesn't want to confine their pup to a crate or simply don't want a crate in their home.

Crate Training

Before you start using the crate as a method of potty training, you should get your dog used to the crate itself. This can be a long process. First, buy a crate that gives your dog plenty of space. If your Lab is a puppy, take into account how big they'll be and how much space they'll need when they're fully grown.

Once you've brought home a properly-sized crate for your lab, fill it with some old pillows or blankets and keep them confined to one side. When your Lab gets to the point of regularly using the crate to do its business, you want to make sure they don't make a mess on their "nest." If you want (it's even probably recommended by most), you can put special pads down to absorb their urine and keep it from spilling over.

Then you want to introduce you Lab to their new crate in the kindest way possible. They should associate the crate with nothing but positive things. Never use the crate as punishment. It will make them reluctant to go in it. Try throwing a few dog treats into the crate. When they go to eat them, shut the door and feed them more treats through the wire. The first couple of weeks, you should move the crate into the room so they have the sense that they're not alone. Chances are they'll probably whine the first few nights. If they do this, simply go over, take them out and see if they need to relieve themselves. Once they do or once they haven't gone for a while, praise them and perhaps give them a treat before putting them back in.

Keep them in the crate any time they're out of your sight to prevent accidents. If your dog's more than six months old, you can leave them in there for about six hours (but not much more). If they're only a few months old, take them out every three hours because dogs that young have trouble holding their bladder.

When you take them out, put them down on a pad directly outside the crate. Wait and keep them there until they do their business, repeating some phrases like "go to the bathroom" to help them associate the command with a green light to go. Do this for a few days and then move the pad into the crate. The next time you take them out, put them directly back in on top of the pad and repeat the command. It may take a while, but they should eventually relieve themselves.

You'll want to supervise them during this as often as possible during the learning the process. Once they can do it without accidents, you can simply switch out pads as often as needed.

This isn't to say that crates should be used all day. At most, they should only be in the crate when they absolutely have to be, like when you're not home or when you have people over. At night, if you're not comfortable with them sleeping with you, you should keep them in the crate with the door closed for the first few weeks. It won't take long for them to realize that this is where they're supposed to sleep. They should start going into it at night by their own will, without you having to put them in there or shut the door.

Outside Training

Teaching your Lab to do its business outside is more complicated than crate or paper training because it requires both you and your dog to operate on a schedule. It also means that you'll have to keep a close eye over what they eat and when they eat. Hopefully, they'll get to the point where they sit by the door or give you a signal when they need to go out. Here's how to get there.

If you're training a puppy (as most of you probably are), you should start potty training immediately. The first few weeks your dogs are home, try to have someone take them out every hour. Keep an eye on them for about ten minutes. Once they relieve themselves, bring them directly back inside. Keep in mind that dogs usually poop twice in each session, so make sure you give them enough time for the second one.

Your dog will pee much more often than they'll go number two. A helpful thing to know is that dogs usually pee about twenty minutes after they drink water. So try to keep track of both when you water and when they go to their water dish, taking them out about twenty minutes after they drink and waiting about ten minutes for them to go.

Another thing you'll want to do is to be consistent in when you feed them. If you're constantly giving them food throughout the day, then food will constantly be moving through their system, increasing the chances for an accident. Feed and water them the same amount at the same times every day. You should also control the times they have access to food. You can do this by leaving the bowl on the ground for as long as it takes for them to get what they need (probably about fifteen minutes) and then picking it up and putting it somewhere that they can't reach it.

When it comes to restricting their access to their water bowl, they should be able to drink water as they need throughout most of the day. However, taking their access to their water bowl away a little while before bedtime can be a good way of decreasing the risk of nighttime accidents. You can probably take away their water dish about two hours before it's time for them to go to bed. If you do this, you should make sure they have access to their water bowl first thing in the morning.

After they do their business, give them praise and repeat certain phrases they can learn to associate with relieving themselves. Make sure you bring them inside as soon as you can after they complete doing their business. Be sure to reward them right away during the first few weeks, starting out with giving them treats and then simply praising them. You don't want to reward or praise your dog after you bring them inside. Instead, you should give them rewards or praise outside immediately after they do their business.

Accidents will happen. As we have discussed before, you should never punish your dog by shoving their nose into their waste. As with anything a dog does, they will only understand the connection to what you do in response to it if your response is done directly after they do it. If they go to the bathroom inside (which they almost certainly will at some point), you should only react if you catch them in the act. If you do, simply pick them up, say a phrase that they can learn to associate with something they shouldn't do, and put them either outside or in time out.

You should supervise your dog as much as you possibly can during the first few weeks of training. If they're going to the bathroom inside half the time and outside half the time, it's going to take them much longer to learn to go outside to relieve themselves. Therefore, you should try to react to every single time they go to the bathroom, putting them out if they go inside and not giving them praise, and giving them treats and praise every time they go to the bathroom outside.

Paper Training

Letting your dog do its business inside is sure to put a lot of people off. But if you're living somewhere that makes taking them out more difficult than you'd like to deal with multiple times a day, it's probably something you'll have to do. Despite this, it's actually much easier to teach your new Lab pup to do its business on a pad than it is to get them to do it inside. With the right training and methods, it only takes about a week to get your new Lab pup to be consistently going to the bathroom in the right place.

Before you can start training your new Lab pup to do its business on a pad inside the house, you'll need to choose a product. There are three main types of different product that you can use for this purpose: pads designed to absorb and keep the area beneath it dry and sanitary, fake grass, and litter boxes built for dogs. All of these have their own benefits. *Litter boxes* allow your dog to relieve itself multiple times over several days before you have to do any cleaning up because of the chemicals in the litter that prevent smell. *Fake-grass pads* benefit you if your dog has some prior training that tells it that grass is where they're supposed to relieve themselves. *Pads* are usually cheaper and are easily cleaned up. None is absolutely better than the other, so it's up to you to decide which one is right for your needs.

You should start paper potty-training your new lab pup the day you bring him home. Like we've discussed in the section about outside potty-training, you should start working right away to get your dog on a feeding schedule, giving them food at the same times every day and then taking it away after fifteen minutes.

Then you'll want to choose a location you can use every day. Your dog is more likely to associate the place they're allowed to go to the bathroom with a location that the surface they're standing on while they do it. Because of this, you want to pick a confined area that doesn't see much traffic. The smaller the better. Ideally, the pad, fake-grass, or litter box should take up the entirety of the area you designate to place them.

Like with outside training, this method of house-breaking requires you to keep a very close eye on your dog for the first couple weeks. Pick them up and put them on the pad or litter box or whatever every hour for about ten minutes and don't let them step off of it. The entire time, you should be repeating and telling them the commands that you've chosen for them to associate with the green light to do their business. Hopefully, this will make them potty on the right surface at least a few times a day. When they do, give them treats and praise them. As you continue doing this, they'll have fewer and fewer accidents and have more and more success with the pad.

Again, if they have accidents, don't punish them. Instead, simply move them over to the pad as quickly as you can, saying the commands such as "no" if you catch them having the accident. If they finish their business on the pad, reward them same as always.

Eventually, your dog should get to the point where they can roam freely around the house without supervision. They should learn how to find the pad when they need it. This allows you to simply change it out once or twice a day as needed. Also, if you think they need to go, consistently using the same word in the first few weeks of training as you watch them potty will help them associate the "time to go" with that specific sound. Eventually, they'll know this sound so well that they'll go to the pad and relieve themselves whenever they hear it.

Top Potty-Training Tips

Before you even start to begin thinking of how to house train your new Lab pup and how to dip yourself and your dog in to the process to begin teaching it to your pup, there are a few things you can do to start getting them in the right mood and mindset to learn the house training procedure on the day you bring them home. First, you should teach them to respect and obey everyone in your home. This can be done first by making sure they are on good grounds with everyone who is regularly going to be in the home with them or at least in the space they're going to regularly inhabit.

One thing you can do right away to ensure this is making sure that your new Lab pup doesn't act aggressively towards any of these people (you should also make sure that your new Lab pup doesn't act aggressively towards strangers, but this requires them acting amiable towards the people they are around day by day first). It also requires that your new lab pup isn't mistreated by anyone who is regularly in your house as well.

Make sure that everyone in your house knows not to act out with anything but kindness and love towards your new friend. If there is a problem with your new Lab pup's behavior with someone in your house for any reason, you can reconcile the two of them by putting them in a room alone together. Make sure this specific person has plenty of treats that can be used to win over the dog's trust. Then, this person can start playing simple games with the new dog. Playing games with small dogs is a quick way to erase any malice the puppy might have towards them. It is largely a trust-building exercise because in order for a dog to play with someone because it requires the dog to believe that they are in a safe environment with that new person.

Making sure your new Lab pup feels comfortable around everyone in your home ensures that they won't ever feel vulnerable when doing their business because the wrong person comes into their space.

Starting at the beginning, you should know that it is possible to start potty-training dogs too early. While it's never too early to start getting them on a schedule and getting them to associate a certain area with going to the bathroom, intensively training a really young dog to go to the bathroom in the right place can be stressful for them. This is because puppies sixteen weeks or younger have little control over their bladders and other bathroom functions. So if your pup is less than four months old, don't set expectations for them that they can't meet.

As we've discussed before, it's important to get your new Lab puppy on a regular feeding schedule as early as you can. Regulating the time your Lab pup eats will automatically regulate the time they feel the need to do their business. To regulate their schedule, give them a set time to eat. This includes putting food in their dish at the same time as well as taking their bowl away about fifteen minutes after you've given to them. They might be a little hungry between meals at first, but it won't take very long at all for them to learn that they need to eat as much as they need to within that fifteen-minute interval.

You should also take your puppy to the area you want them to do their business in right after when they wake up in the morning and right before when they go to bed at night. You should also take them to that area about thirty minutes after meals as well as about twenty minutes after they drink any water.

You should also make sure you're always encouraging them to do their business in the same spot. Moving their pad around to different locations or taking them outside to different areas will confuse them as to exactly where they should relieve themselves. Keeping the pad in the same spot or taking them out to the same spot will prompt them to go more easily for two reasons: first, the familiarity of the location will relax them as they get more and more into a routine; second, if you bring them to the same place to relieve themselves repeatedly for a good amount of time, the area will build up with their business and it will develop a scent about it that gives them the green light and makes them more comfortable to go. The smell probably won't be palpable to you, but they will be able to sense it.

When training your new Lab pup to do their business outside, if that is what you've chosen to do, make sure you stay with them the entire time they're outside until they're been successfully trained. This is an important thing to do because it makes you new Lab pup feel more comfortable being outside. Also, it makes sure they don't have a chance to run off or get lost because you left them outside when they didn't know better than to run off. Lastly, it ensures you have the chance to watch them to make sure they do their business before you let them back in.

Another good tip for when you're either first starting to or are still in the process of training your pup to do its business outside is to watch them the entire time they're outside and to stay out there with them. Then you keep watching them until they've done their business. As soon as they've done their business, give them either a treat as well as praise or simply just praise depending on what stage they are in their potty-training process. After you've either given them a treat and praise or simply just praise, bring them back inside immediately after they've done their business. This will do two things. The first thing it does is that it makes them associate the praise you're giving them with doing their business outside in the right place. The second thing it does is that it makes the associate getting to go back inside with doing their business outside in the right place.

Another thing you can do to stop them from getting desensitized from the joy they get from getting praise or a treat or both is to give them some other reward for going to the bathroom outside or in the general right place. There are a few different types of awards you can give them in this situation. The rewards that I am going to suggest require that you spend time with your new Lab pup and give them some form of extra attention. One of these awards is simply to take them on a walk in a new environment. This can be as simple as taking them on a walk around the neighborhood your house is in. It can also come in the form of taking them out to a dog park or somewhere new where they can run around and play and have fun without being confined by a leash. It can also come in the form of taking them on a short walk in a nearby forest, either behind your house or close enough to where you live that you can get there on foot in a short amount of time.

When trying to house-train your new Lab pup, you should be aware of the specific needs that your Labrador has as a breed. As they get bigger and stronger, their bladders and the muscles that control them will get bigger and stronger as well. This means that, while it can prevent most accidents, taking you Labrador outside every single hour for ten minutes might end up confusing them because Labs don't need to go to the bathroom as often as some other dogs do. So when you bring them outside when they don't have to go to the bathroom too frequently, it might confuse them as to whether being outside is the sure sign that they are free to go to the bathroom. They should automatically associate being outside with the green light that tells them it's alright to go to the bathroom. Labs are smarter than most other dogs so they'll pick up on this quicker than other breeds will. Still, they don't learn as people do. Be patient with them.

What to Know About Your Labrador's Behavior and How to Control It

L ike all dog breeds, Labrador Retrievers have certain behaviors that are unique to them. In Labradors, you'll see a conglomeration of traits that you probably won't find in any other dog breed. They have specific needs that you should know how to meet. Knowing what traits are common in Labradors and which traits aren't can help you identify the behaviors that are naturally occurring as well as the behaviors that can help you identify certain problems with their physical and mental health.

In this section, I will name and discuss some traits that are definitely behavior traits you should know about your new friend. I will also name and discuss some behavioral traits that might seem innocuous but are still probably things you should be aware of and know how to control. Even small traits can lead to stress for you and your new Lab pup. This stress can manifest in aggressive or other types of unwanted behavior, not eating, or a loss of sleep for both you and your pup.

Most of these traits are inherent in the Labrador's genetic and evolutionary makeup. it is neither the fault of your dog or the fault of yourself as an owner that your Labrador is displaying these traits. As a result, it is important that you approach correcting these behaviors with both compassion and kindness both for yourself as an owner and for your Labrador as an animal who hasn't really done anything wrong.

Basic Labrador Traits and the Causes of Unwanted Behavior

One of the most recognizable traits of the Labrador Retriever as a dog breed in its kindness and gentleness. Most know or are at least familiar with the Labrador's amiable expression. You don't often see a Labrador who has a scary or negative expression on its face because they're so well known for their good mood. This is part of the reason why that Labradors are often recommended for families that have children because they are often not likely to bite them or act out towards them in other aggressive ways. If your Labrador (or any type of dog breed, for that matter) is acting out aggressively, there's probably something wrong. This isn't to say that you're necessarily a bad owner. It may be that their unwanted behavior is the product of how someone else is acting or treating them or from some other thing that is completely out of your control. It's very possible that they're acting this way because of something that happened to them before you brought them home. It also may be the product of the way someone else is treating them when you're not around.

If your Labrador is exhibiting some kind of aggression or other types of unwanted behavior, you should start figuring out why they're acting that way either immediately or as soon as you possibly can. There are things you may be doing that is causing your new Lab pup to act this way. The list of possible things that could be causing them to act this way is far too long for me to list here, but I will include an example of a case I hear of a while back that embodies some of the more common mistakes that good, loving owners make when otherwise treating their dogs kindly and generally doing everything else right.

A few years ago, I encountered a Labrador that was acting out aggressively towards other people. The owner would put them on a leash and take them out for a walk. On these walks, his Labrador would act out, growling and barking and lunging at certain strangers who would walk by. Also, at home, certain people would come over and the dog would run from them, distance themselves from these certain people and act out towards them with hostility by running around and barking and growling at them.

When I first encountered this Labrador and her owner, I was initially very confused at her behavior. Her owner seemed very put together, calm, and seemed to treat her and other people with respect and kindness. Furthermore, the dog seemed well groomed and well fed and put together. So I spent a while talking to him as to how he was at home with her and which things he often did with her. I was able to point out two problematic things that were causing her to act that way.

First, the man was a big sports fan. He often spent hours a day watching sports games on the TV, specifically hockey and football. He told me that he often got very passionate about the games, perhaps too much so. I asked him to describe to me how he acted while watching them, and he told me, with a bit of embarrassment, that he yelled and screamed and cursed at his TV when things weren't going the way he liked. I asked him if the dog was present during these times, and he said she was. The problem here was that he didn't know that, even if he was not acting this way towards his dog, she was still picking up on his vibe and energy while he was watching these games. Surely, all his yelling and noise got her attention. As he got more and more excited about whatever he was acting out towards, in the same way did she get more and more excited and wired up. The difference is that he, as an emotionally stable human, was able to let go of these powerful emotions after the game ended. But his dog often didn't know that it was time to let go of these emotions as well as how to let go of them, hence that aggression stayed in her and caused her to act out towards other people.

The other thing that was causing this aggression in her took place on the walks he took with her almost daily. He'd take her around the city for about an hour before going back up to his apartment. At the end of these walks, he'd let her off the leash and let her run up the stairs by herself. Then he'd follow her up and wrestle with her at the top of the stairs by the door. While this may seem innocuous, in the sense of how the dog's psyche works, it was very significant. Dogs have an idea of their home space (the apartment at the top of the stairs in this case) as their own and something that must be defended at all cost.

By letting her off the leash and letting her run up the stairs, she was taught to retake her home at the end of each of these walks. To make things worse, his wrestling with her was to her a form of fighting for the home. So she was put in this perpetual mindset of having to reclaim and fight for her home every time she went on these walks. This wired her up and made her very defensive of both her owner and her home, which caused her to act out to people she viewed, for whatever reason, as a threat to either of these things.

That story is a good example of how an otherwise good and kind Labrador owner can evoke some kind of aggressive behavior in their Labrador from the simple reason of not understanding both the nature of the dog's mind and how they pick up on the behavior and vibe of both their owners and others around them. So if your dog is displaying some kind of unwanted behavior and you don't know why, I encourage you to analyze everything you do with your dog or the things you do while your dog is present and think about those activities in terms of how they may affect your dog. You cannot cure a dog of any behavior when you don't know the root problem.

Curbing Biting, Licking, and Aggressive Behavior

Biting (often play-biting) and licking are two of the most common problems in all types of dog breeds. In this section, we'll start by looking at why dogs bite and what you can do to curb it. Then we'll move onto biting and describe and cover the same things.

All puppies bite people, either strangers or the person they're closest to you. A lot of owners don't see play-biting as a huge problem, but a lot of people are very put off at the idea of a dog covering their hand with saliva and all the germs that come with it. To keep yourself from putting people who might come into contact with your dog with this problem, it's useful to know just how to stop your dog from doing it.

Play-biting is common in dogs up to the age of about eighteen months. While it can be cute and non-painful when the dog is very tiny, this can change when the dog gets bigger and stronger. Now, your dog is biting in the same way that it did when it was a little puppy, only now it hurts and it's more than just an occasional nuisance.

There are a couple of main reasons that puppies bite. The first is that they have new teeth coming in, and sometimes this can be quite uncomfortable for them. Biting can help decrease the uncomfortableness they feel as their new teeth come in as well as toughen up their teeth. Biting also serves as a way for them to play and manipulate objects. If you try to get your dog to not bite anything, you're probably going to have a rough time because biting is the way they eat and experience the world. So it's very important that you supply them with an object that they're allowed to bite such as ropes, stuffed animals, bones, or chew-toys.

Some biting is to be expected from your new Lab pup. But there are a lot of reasons that your new Lab up might be either biting more than you'd like or continuing to bite a lot after they're biting at an age where they're older than they should be. A lot of times this is because they're getting more excited than they can handle and it causes them to do things that they have some idea that they shouldn't. In fact, most problems that people experience with puppies is often due to them being more excited than they know how to handle.

When a puppy bites because they're over-excited, there's usually a few things that come along with it. These things include growling or snarling, running around and stopping and going very quickly in jolting fashion, nipping at you or someone else in a very quick, hyper manner (the zoomies), ripping your clothes or their toys, fast wagging of the tail, or spinning around very quickly.

So what should you do if your puppy is overly excited? Well, if it's clear that they're overly-excited, there are a few things you should do immediately. First, you should look at how you're playing with your Lab puppy and end the game as soon as possible. Second, put the Lab puppy in a space that is quiet and free from distractions or anything else that could possibly get them excited. Also, if you can or if you want to or feel like you need to, you can leave the space and leave them by themselves for a little while. This will result in a lack of stimuli for your Lab pup and is a quick way to get them to calm down. After they've gotten calmed down and they're not nipping or acting out anymore, you should analyze what you were doing with your lab pup before they starting biting and acting overly excited and search for things that may have triggered it. Take an honest look at the situation and think of what you can do differently in the future to prevent this. This doesn't mean that, if your Lab puppy got overly excited at a certain game, that you can or should never play that game with them again. It simply means that the next time you play that game with your Lab pup, you should tone down the intensity of the game you're playing.

You should know how to tell the difference as to whether or not your pup's biting is the result of being overly excited or whether it is the result of them being aggressive. Even if your pup is loud and running around a lot, chances are it's from simply being overly excited. Something you should know about aggression is that it's almost always a result of your dog being afraid. When a dog is aggressive, it usually gets very still or at most will pace or make short movements, always going back into the same posture and focusing on the same point. Dogs that afraid of something don't run all over the room. Another sure way to tell if your dog is aggressive is the position of their tail. Usually, it will be between their legs. Often a scared and aggressive dog will act scared and fearfully, and as a result, they'll hide in corners or beneath furniture or freeze in place completely.

If you catch your dog being aggressive towards you or anyone, immediately isolate them from the situation. Take them into a safe place where there aren't a lot of people or things that could scare them in any sense. Try getting some of their favorite treats and hold them out to them or throw them on the ground. Do not try to pet your dog or move near it quickly. Make your motions very slow and gentle and speak to your dog in a comforting tone. It might take a while for your dog to calm down and trust you. After you've gotten them to calm down, keep them in a safe place where they can relax. Then you should take an honest assessment of the situation and what made them scared and caused them to act aggressively. Do everything you can to avoid putting your dog in that situation again and educate anyone who was involved not to act in whatever way they did towards your lab again.

If your dog is acting aggressively and there doesn't seem to be any obvious reason for it, take them to the vet. It is possible that they have some sort of injury or condition that is causing them pain. Dogs can't tell us that they aren't feeling good or that they're in pain. When dogs are hurt or they have something that's causing them pain, they often act out aggressively in fear of being hurt more.

Licking is almost never the product of aggression, which makes it far less worrying than biting. But having a dog that licks excessively or obsessively can be a burden. When a dog licks you, all the bacteria in their mouth (which probably has thousands, if not millions, of contaminates) gets onto your skin, which is pretty gross to think about.

Dogs lick for two main reasons. The first reason they lick is also found among wolves and other animals in the wild. These wild animals lick because it shows submission to the dominant animals in the group. They also lick because it shows affection towards their peers in the group. So, when a dog licks you, there's a good chance that they're doing it as a sign of affections and that you're in control and they trust you.

But dogs sometimes also lick because of the simple reason that they like the taste of your skin. If you don't know why, do a simple experiment and lick your arm. It tastes salty, right? Your sweat glands produce water that is very high in salt, sodium, and other minerals. Dogs usually like this salty taste and so that's why they like to lick you. A simple way of getting your dog to stop licking you is to get them a salt lick. Most dog food doesn't have a lot of sodium, and so most dogs are at least a little low in sodium. Getting them a salt rock or other types of salt licks that they can lick whenever they want is a good way to increase your dog's sodium levels and decrease the amount that they feel the need to lick you.

When a dog licks because of affection, it makes them feel good. Their brains produce endorphins that evoke feelings of pleasure and trust. One sure way to combat this form of licking is to eliminate the endorphins they get from licking. So how do we decrease the endorphins? It's simple; never react positively to licking. Licking should never be rewarded. If your Lab licks you, ignore them. Talk to them in a stern voice and don't praise them. You can even get up and move to the other room. This won't work right away. It might take them a while to learn that licking results in things that aren't positive and are even things that they don't like. This is why it's important to be consistent. Don't budge. Don't give in and reward them for it. Make it clear to them that if they lick you, they will not be rewarded.

Curbing Barking

All Labradors bark. It's just going to happen. But there's a difference between a Lab that barks occasionally at understandably intense stimuli and a dog that barks constantly. A Lab that barks too much can be very disruptive to not only the owners of the dog but also to the neighbors and anyone who might come over to your home.

Knowing how to effectively and kindly stop a dog from barking is one of the best things you can do for both the atmosphere of your home as well as the relationship your dog has both with you and as well as everyone your dog comes into contact with.

It's important that your dog knows when it is okay to bark and as well as when it's important for them to be quiet. If your dog barks excessively, it's your job as someone who chose to bring your dog into your neighborhood to keep it from disturbing and annoying those around your home. As soon as you realize that your dog is barking too much, you should start working to reverse that habit immediately before it becomes deeply ingrained into your dog's personality. One way you can curb barking is to teach your dog commands that tell it to speak and tell it to be quiet.

The first step to curbing your Labrador's excessive barking is understanding why it's barking so much. There can be a variety of reasons why your dog is barking too much. I'll list them shortly below.

Territorial Barking: This is barking that stems from the need your dog feels to protect you as well as their home. This comes in the form of barking at animals as well as strangers who may come into or close to their home. My Labrador, who has a yard to run around in without a fence (I live very far out in the country), often barks at night at wild animals such as coyotes or raccoons.

Lonely Barking: Dogs function best and are their happiest when they're surrounded by other animals or people that they feel close to (think of the term "pack"). When Labradors are alone for much of the day, it tends to make them very unhappy. They like to be with other dogs or people. Like us, they need others to have a sense of fulfillment. When they're not happy, they tend to bark out of a lack of happiness.

"Hello" Barking: This is probably the healthiest form of barking. Barking is basically how dogs talk. When they meet someone new, whether they're happy to meet them or suspicious of them, it's their instinct to bark at them.

Separation Anxiety Barking: This often takes place in very young puppies. When a dog is very young (around four months or younger), their natural instinct is to want to be around their mother or whoever is taking care of them. So they sometimes have a real problem with being alone, especially when they're about to go to sleep at night. We won't cover this here but in one of the other sections of this chapter.

Attention-Seeking Barking: Sometimes Labradors bark for attention. This can vary as to which attention level is so low that your dog feels the need to bark. If your Labrador is used to a high level of attention, then it's going to take less of a lack of attention to get them to bark.

Pain Barking: Sometimes, when dogs have medical issues that cause them pain, dogs will bark to voice their discontent.

The best thing you can do to curb excessive barking is to figure out the cause of excessive barking and remove it from the equation. Along with this, there is something you don't want to do, which is to encourage barking in any way. Encouraging barking, even when you don't mean to, will make it very confusing for your Labrador when you try to curb their barking.

You can start by making sure your dog is very active. Do your best to make sure they're tired by the time they go to bed at night. Go in walks, play games with them, or do anything else you can to burn them out of having energy by the end of the day. A dog that is kept up all day will have a lot of energy when it gets dark and it is time to go to bed. A tired dog is a quiet dog.

You should also try to make sure that your dog has company. The lonely dog is a loud dog. They act out for attention. Make sure your dog gets attention and is satisfied with their environment.

One thing you should never do is to reward your dog when they're barking. Often good-meaning Labrador owners accidentally encourage excessive barking by thinking their dog needs to be coaxed into being quiet. If you think that your dog is barking because it's lonely, don't go out and try to give it company right away. Do it the next day or sometime when they're not barking. If you go out and try to comfort your barking dog, you're rewarding their behavior. This will teach them to bark to get rewards, which you do not want.

You also should not act negatively towards your dog for barking. Don't shout or scream at them for barking. This will add to their excitement and perhaps will make them bark more.

If you find your dog barking excessively, there are a few things you can do to try to stop it right away. You can throw them a toy or give them a nice snack to avert their attention. You can also command them to sit down, come, or do any other thing that will get their attention off whatever they're barking at.

As a long-term solution when none of these reasons seem to explain why your dog is barking and it's a chronic problem, you can train your dog commands of when to speak and be quiet.

How to Deal with Separation Anxiety

Separation Anxiety is one of the most common problems in Labradors. It doesn't just take place in puppies, but dogs of all ages. It can also manifest itself in dogs of any age. Separation Anxiety can be very destructive, not just to your dogs physical and mental health but also can be a detriment to their mental health. If they freak out when they're left alone, they can do some serious damage to your furniture and other objects around the house. You've probably seen photos of dogs sulking around cushions, pillows, trash bags, or other things they've ripped apart. Sometimes this kind of destruction can be caused by your Lab's simple bad behavior, but more often it is caused by the distress they feel when their owners are not around. In this section, we'll cover the causes on Separation Anxiety as well as things you can do for your dog to eliminate this behavior.

This kind of behavior could be because they don't know which objects around them are okay to chew on and which are not. But more often it's simple separation anxiety. A good way to determine which it is by watching how your dog behaves as you're getting ready to leave the house without them. If they seem calm and uninterested, it may not be separation anxiety that's causing their behavior. However, if your dog acts sad or nervous when you are getting ready to leave, that's a sign of separation anxiety. Some dogs with separation anxiety will even try to stop their owners from leaving. Another way to tell whether or not your Lab has separation anxiety is to wait outside after you leave and listen for the sounds inside. If your dog is whining or barking directly after you've left them alone, that's a good sign that they have separation anxiety. They may also go to the bathroom inside the house when left alone. Some dogs may even try to escape the area they're confined in if their separation anxiety is too much for them to handle.

There are a few different causes of separation anxiety. It is known that dogs that come from a shelter or some type of abusive environment are more likely to develop separation anxiety. Another common cause of separation anxiety is the loss of another pet or of an important person who was previously around their home a lot. It can also develop when a dog's schedule changes drastically. For example, if they're used to being left alone from seven until three and then you switch to second shift and are gone from three to twelve, they could get thrown off of what they're used to and become very confused as to when their owner is coming back. Another thing that can cause separation anxiety is when they've moved from one place to another which puts the dog in a new environment and confuses them. It can also be caused by a new person moving into the home, putting them on edge by having a person they don't know being around a lot. It can also just be a product of having a dog that's too young to know better.

Also, when a dog is left in a room without something to entertain itself with, it can cause destruction, go to the bathroom, and try to escape out of boredom alone. If your dog is behaving like this and is locked in a room without a window, toys, or a friend to play with for an extended amount of time, try putting them into a place where they have something that can occupy their mind before you decide it's separation anxiety.

There are a few things you can do to help your dog with separation anxiety. If your dog's separation anxiety isn't too bad (but still a problem), something you can do is to do things that make them associate being alone with something that makes them happy. One possible course of action is to give them some sort of delicious food when you leave. You should give them enough of the treat that it will take them a while to eat all of it. Another thing you can do to help your Lab with separation anxiety is to get a kind of toy that requires the dog to work to get to the inside. You can put some sort of a tasty treat inside it that they'll have to work to get out. It can be a type of chew toy that requires them to chew on it for quite a while (maybe even a few hours) before they can get to the tasty food inside. This will do two things; first, it will help them associate the tasty treat with being alone for an extended amount of time; second, it will give them something to entertain themselves with while you're gone, helping them get their mind off the fact that they're alone.

If your dog's separation anxiety is more severe and is causing serious problems both to your home and to your Lab's health, there are some more time-consuming steps you should take to rectify this problem. One thing you can do is to decrease the time they're alone until you find a period that they're comfortable with. If you aren't capable of coming back to your home this often for whatever reason, try to find a family member or a friend that can stop by every so often to visit your dog and put them at ease. As they get used to being alone for these short periods of time, slowly start extending the period they are in the home alone until they get to the point where they can be alone for the entire time you have to be gone.

Teaching Your Labrador How to Fetch

W hen you think of a Labrador and their owner playing in a park, you probably imagine them playing fetch. Fetch is one of the best, most classical game you can play with your dog. It's an incredibly good bonding experience as well as being a great way to keep your dog fit and active. But most dogs don't know how to play fetch, and probably as many owners don't know how to teach them to. Everyone loves a Lab that can play fetch. They're usually friendly, well-adjusted, and knowing how to fetch gives them a sure way to bond with anyone who might cross into your life. In this section, we'll go over when to start teaching your dog how to fetch, the basic training methods you can start with, and some techniques you can do to perfect the game.

Basic Methods to Start With

To be honest, a dog is really never too young to start learning something. However, it should be done in the right way with realistic expectations. Young Labs have short attention spans and, especially in the first few months, may not have the cognitive ability or the energy to learn a game as intensive and fetching. Don't get me wrong, it's much easier to teach young dogs than old dogs, but, if you do start training your Lab pup when it's only a few months old, be prepared to spend more time training them than you would if they were around six months old.

Dogs will never know how to fetch unless you teach them how to correctly. It's not instinctual. While they are often automatically inclined to chase after and run off with something you've thrown, there's nothing that tells them to bring it back to you. Teaching a dog how to return what you've thrown to you is the hardest part of teaching a dog how to fetch. Every step along the path to mastering the game of fetch is a challenge for your dog. They have to learn and think and change their own behavior.

Something you can do to start the process of teaching them to fetch from a very young age is by simply throwing a ball, stick, or another toy, waiting for them to pick it up, and then chasing them as they run around with it. The game "chase" is something dogs love to do and will almost always do automatically. They love to chase. However, if your dog doesn't seem interested, something you can do is to offer them a reward for retrieving the object, practicing throwing it near and far over and over again until they develop an interest in it. When the pick it up, give them a treat. Even if he just goes over near it and smells it without picking it up, give him a treat and award them for showing interest in it. Do this over and over again until they run over and pick up the object every single time. If you're having a hard time getting them interested, try restricting their movement right after you throw it. Like teenagers, the fastest thing you can do to get a dog interested in something is to make them think you don't want them to do it.

Now that you've taught your dog to chase after and pick up the object consistently, it's important to do as much as you can to keep them focused. A big problem people run into when teaching their dog how to fetch is that the dog just wants to grab the object and run around with it. It might be funny at first, but soon you'll get tired of chasing your Lab around trying to get the object back. So a good way to help keep your dog within your reach is to use a long leash or rope to reel them in when they get too excited and simply don't want to give the object back to you. If you don't have a leash or a rope long enough, something else you can do is offer them a treat when they're running around with the object. Usually, when your Lab sees the food, they'll drop the object and come over to get the treat. If they try to pick up the object and run with it, gently pull on the rope and then start running or walking in the other direction. When you do this, your dog will come over to you.

When they come over to you, praise them and get them a treat. Doing this will encourage them to come over to you in the future.

Another problem many people run into when teaching their Labs how to fetch is that their dogs want to play tug-of-war with you for the object. Most dogs love this game, and often they'll hold onto it with every muscle they have for a very long time. In the same way as above, you can offer them a treat to get them to let it go. Put the treat right by their nose so they can smell it. Usually, they'll let go of the object to get the treat.

Mastering the Game

After you can get your dog to consistently pick up the treat and you have a way of getting it back with ease, you can start training them to do the hardest part of fetching which is retrieving.

There's a big difference between a dog that knows how to fetch and a dog that can only run after an object and claim it as its own. Retrieving is going to take the longest amount of time to train your dog how to do than any other part of the process of learning fetching will. When you first start trying to teach them this, it can be a very long and hard and frustrating process. But it's important to keep your cool and to treat your dog with nothing but kindness, patience, and compassion. Learning how to fetch should not be a stressful experience for your dog. If they feel nervous or distressed, it will make all of your play time a time they don't want to be apart of. It can also manifest itself in other behavioral problem at home or with other dogs or people.

When you first start trying to teach them this stage of fetching, they probably won't have any interest in bringing the object back at all. What can help you here is to get a second toy to get their attention and make them drop the object. You can do this either by throwing it or teasing them with it. Once they've expressed interest in the second toy, they'll likely drop the first toy. You can try going over and picking it up, keeping their interest in the second toy if you can. This way your Lab has no toys while you have both, which you can use in the exact same way if they don't want to bring the first toy back at all again. This also gets your lab used to the idea of running back to you after they've picked up the object. Any time your Lab comes back over to you after picking up the object, even if they hold onto the toy or try running away again, give them a treat. It makes them associate getting a treat with the act of bringing the object back to you.

As you try to teach them the act of retrieving, call their name when right after they pick up the object. It helps if your dog already knows and can consistently obey the command for "come" in other circumstances. Teaching a dog to fetch should usually be done only after a dog has been taught how to do other commands. It helps reduce the chances that your Lab will run away from you or be generally difficult while trying to teach them to fetch.

If your dog begins to bring the object back over to you but drops it before they come over to you all the way, say "bring it here" or "give it here." Do this every time they retrieve it, whether they bring it all the way back to you or not. Also, if they drop it, go over and pick it up and then walk back to the place where you were standing before throwing the object again. This will help them when they don't understand. Once you've done it enough, only throw the object from a certain area and that's where you need to be with the object to throw it again.

You should also make sure that you're playing catch with something your dog likes and has interest in. If you get a random stick that they haven't shown interest in, it's going to be hard to get them interested enough in it to go over and pick it up. If you're having trouble getting your dog interested, experiment with different types of toys such as bones or small balls until you've found something they want to go get and don't want to let go of.

Leash Training Your Labrador

P roper leash training is one of the most important things you can teach your dog. It should also be one of the first things you try to teach your dog. A dog that knows how to properly behave when they're on the leash can be the difference between a dog whose walks are tiring and stressful and a dog whose walks are relaxing and casual. It also saves you from embarrassment from walking a dog that barks at people or tries to flee from you when you're out in public. You can always tell when a dog hasn't been properly leash trained. They're always pulling their owners with a lot of force and stopping to sniff things with no regards to what their owner wants to do, causing their owner to have to either won't until their done or to yank them with what is probably more force than they would like to use.

In this section, we'll go over why dogs misbehave on the leash, the difference between good leash behavior and bad leash behavior, and what you can do to train your dog to behave correctly on the leash when out and about. Following the steps in this section should teach your dog how to keep going without you trying to pull them, how to go around corners and follow your direction, and how to walk by people and other animals without misbehaving.

Bad Leash Behavior

One of the most common problems with leash behavior is pulling on the leash. The reasons why Labs pull on leashes is very simple. Like all dogs, Labs have a natural instinct to not give in to pressure. Instead, they almost always feel the need to pull against it. When they're restricted by a leash, they're going to want to go places outside of the space they're allotted. They also want to get to where they're going faster (most humans move a lot slower when they're walking than dogs would like). When labs are on the leash, they're usually not focused on the human on the other end. They're in their old world. This can lead to some nerve-racking problems such as choking which can scare owners since their dogs cough, heave, and gasp. But this reaction usually sounds worse than it really is.

Another problem people often experience when walking their dogs is that their Labs like to bite or chew on the leash. How often labs do this depend on the individual dog. Some dogs do it just because they like it. Other dogs only do it because they're overly nervous or excited. Another reason Labs chew or bite on the leash is because they want attention, as biting or chewing on the leash often makes their owners react in some way.

A dog that isn't leash-trained will also do a lot of stopping. The root of this problem is similar to the problem that causes dogs to pull on the leash. They do this because they don't have a sense of a connection with the human on the other end of the leash. Again, they're in their old little world, and, when they see or smell something interesting, their natural inclination is a powerful desire to stop and observe it.

How to Fix Bad Leash Behavior

Something you should be able to do before ever taking them out on a walk is the ability to take their attention no matter where the two of you are. They should be able to react to their name and obey commands no matter what place they find themselves in. You can start practicing this by calling their name in your home or in any other place that doesn't have any distractions. After they can do this consistently, try going out into the yard or into another place that has slightly more distractions. As they get better and better at doing this easily, move them into bigger, busier environments. This is the first step in correcting bad behavior.

One of the other things you should do early in the process is to learn to control the environments you take your Lab on walks on as best as you can. Taking them on walks with loud traffic can make it harder for them to hear you when you need to give them some sort of commands. It can also cause them to be over-excited and unable to obey your commands or calm down. Also, depending on whether or not your lab is trained to be calm and comfortable around dogs, you should make sure you're not taking them into an environment where they might be overwhelmed with and act out at other dogs. If you do find yourself approaching a dog and your lab is not reacting well or isn't ready for being around another dog, go in a half circle around the dog to keep the dog and your Lab at a safe distance from one another.

If your dog has a problem with barking while the two of you are on walks, there's probably a simple, easy to fix reason for this. Most excessive barking is usually caused by simply having too much energy. If you find your dog barking at people or other animals, try playing a game that will wear him out before you leave the house. You can play chase, tug-of-war, or any other kind of game that will make them tired after a while. Exercising not only keeps your Lab in good health, but it also has a calming effect on them after they've done it. It takes a lot of energy to act out with bad behavior. A tired dog is a calm dog.

A good way to stop your dog from pulling is by enacting strict leash discipline. For example, the only time your dog should be allowed to move ahead of you is when the leash isn't strained. As soon as it tightens, stop walking and don't budge. Wait for the dog to move back a little and loosen the leash before letting the two of you move forward again. It may take a while for your Lab to change his behavior by doing this, but it's worth it once they learn. If you're having a particularly hard time changing your lab's behavior, you can come up with a command to say every time you have to stop for pulling on the leash. Eventually, this should get to the point where your Lab will stop pulling on the leash from that command alone.

It is also a very big help if you've previously trained your dog to respond to basic commands. This is because, if your dog stops to smell or look at something, one thing you can do to rectify their behavior is to ask them to do a basic command to get their attention off whatever object they're smelling or looking at.

Another thing you can do to get your dog to stop their bad leash behavior is to train them to be aware and attentive to you on their walks. All you have to do to get this behavior instilled in them is to carry a good amount of treats with you while you're on walks with them. Pay attention to where they're looking. Every time they look back at you on the walk, give them a treat or a reward. If your dog isn't looking at you at all, call their name and give them a treat when they look at you. This gets your Lab to associate looking at you with the pleasure of getting a treat. It can make them, over time, if done consistently, very in tune with whoever is walking them. It can make them very respectful and thoughtful as to what the person who's walking them is doing.

If your dog has a problem with biting or chewing on their leash while walking, one thing you can do is to take the focus off the act of chewing or biting on the leash and replacing it with something else. Find some other behavior to reward, such as certain kinds of walks. Of course, this means that your dog must already know other types of walks before this kind of discipline can work. Another thing you can do to fix this behavior if your Lab doesn't know any other kinds of commands to replace with leash biting or chewing is to take away the reason they're biting or chewing on a leash. This can be done by walking them with two leashes. When the Lab starts to bit or chew on one leash, drop it and use the other. Once the leash goes loose, they likely won't be interested in chewing or biting on it anymore.

Maintaining Your Labrador's Behavior

I t is not much good to train your dog how to behave well and how to do all these commands and tricks if they lose the ability how to do it after a couple of months. You can't spend a few months training your dog and then just drop off the amount of effort you put in. This is because training does a couple things for a Lab. First, it gives it order and structure. It makes it feel like it has a purpose, and Labs who feel as though they have a purpose are much happier and much more well behaved than those that don't. Second, it keeps your dog in good physical health by making sure it has plenty of exercises. Third, it provides both of you with a bonding experience. The dynamic you form with your dog by teaching them commands as well as having them execute commands keeps the two of you on the same page. You become very in tune as to what their current mood is and your Lab becomes very in tune to your mood.

Maintaining Good Behavior

An important part of learning good behavior is that it instills in the Lab the difference between which behaviors are good and which behaviors are bad. Of course, you don't go through and teach them every single bad behavior. Instead, you give them a certain command that you can use at any time when they exhibit bad behavior. It's important that you use this consistently. The longer you use it, the more receptive they will be towards it. It will make them stop the behavior quicker and quicker as time goes on. Do not let bad behavior slide by, no matter how inane it may seem. Once they get away with something, they then think it's alright. When they think something's alright, they do it again. Not only do they do it again, but they then push it further. It can be easy to slip into the habit of letting some of your dog's seemingly unimportant bad behavior slip by because you think it isn't a big deal, and that one incident probably isn't. but once you've let it slip once, it's easier to let it slip the next time. Also, it can cause stress to your Lab because you're sending them mixed messages. If something seems okay to do half the time and not okay the other half of the time, they won't know which one to do and that can cause distress when you do scold them for it.

Because of what we've described above, you always need to be giving your dog feedback, and it shouldn't just be in response to bad behavior. Instead, just like you discourage bad behavior, you should always be encouraging good behavior. When your Lab showcases its training or does something right or really well, they should know that what they've just done is good. This doesn't mean you have to always give them a few treats, but it does mean that you should show your appreciation of the good behavior.

You should also exercise the right kind of behavior in the right times and places. If there's one place you should be exercising your control over your dog's behavior, it should be in an exciting, stimulating, or challenging situations. If you bring your dog to a dog park, and there's a dog there that your Lab isn't acting positively towards, you should tell them to sit or get their attention, keeping their behavior in check and making sure they can continuously focus on you in these kinds of environments. Another place your dog's good behavior should be tested is in the home when you have company over. You should always make sure your dog is calm and non-aggressive towards anyone who walks in your house. If they are, you should immediately get them under control and put them into a different room where they can calm down.

One of the most important things you can do to maintain your Lab's good behavior is to make sure that they are healthy and happy. When a dog is getting too little of something it needs or too much of something it doesn't, this excess or deficiency can often manifest itself in bad behavior. There are many different aspects of your dog's life you should keep a close eye on to keep them balanced.

First, you should make sure your dog is getting enough food and water and general nutrients. Second, you should make sure your dog is getting enough social activity, either with you or other animals. You really don't want to leave your dog alone for long periods of time (more than four hours) if you can help it. If you don't have a choice in this matter, put it in a yard with plenty of space or a dog daycare center. If you have no choice but to keep your dog inside, they should at the very least have a window to look out of. Also, if they have to be inside, give them a dog toy designed to keep their interest such as a food-holder they have to chew through to get the snack or some sort of puzzle. You should also make sure your dog is living in an environment that is as stress-free as it can possibly be. Recall the story I told of a dog who was on edge because of how her owner reacted to sports games. As far as you can help it, you should make sure your home is calm and quiet.

Maintaining Your Lab's Training

Like how a car needs to have oil changes and tune-ups to keep running well, in the same way does a Lab need constant upkeep to keep their training sharp and crisp. You should have your

Lab practicing its tricks daily, even if it's only a few. A good way to remember to do this is to have a ritual you do with your dog every day. When you feed them, you can have them sit patiently while you put down the food and then have them speak before they eat. Also, when letting them in and out of the house, you can practice the "come" and "sit" and "speak" commands. If you're into exercising and have the time for it, you can bring your dog on a nightly walk and have them practice good leash training as well as obedience around things that may excite or over-stimulate them. You can also take them to a dog park or open field and play a daily game of fetch with them, practicing come, sit, and go commands in between throws. Maintaining this training is also a good way to make sure your Lab stays the same.

Another good thing you can do to maintain your Lab's training is to keep challenging them.

Besides the basic commands and games, there are also hundreds of different games and commands you can teach to your dog beside the ones we've covered. Constantly teaching your dog different commands has a few positive benefits. First, it keeps their mind sharp by challenging them with new things they don't know how to do. Second, it keeps a nice, strong bond between the two of you by ensuring you spend so much time with them giving them your attention. Third, it keeps them focused on you. One of the worst things that can happen in terms of training your dog is for your dog to stop being attentive towards you. This can come about because you're not practicing your commands enough or because your dog gets bored with certain things. Constantly adding more commands makes your dog excited and interested in the time you spend together.

Besides teaching your Lab new skills, you can also practice the same old skills in new situations and environments. If your dog has mastered the basic commands at home, take them on hikes and into new places they haven't been to before. Get their interest peaked and then practice those old commands in places they're excited to be in. Practice taking him around people and practice those commands with them there. This will increase your Lab's attention span. When a dog's in an environment with lots of interesting things around, it's harder for them to focus on what you're saying. So bringing them into these kinds of environments and practicing these skills will make them a lot more attentive towards you and, as a result, easier to control.

If your dog does lose its training, don't challenge them too much. Slowly move your way back to the basics to see what your lab's skill level is. Once you find it, work up from there. It's not necessarily a bad thing that your dog loses training, it just means you get to spend more time with them in order to retrain them. They'll almost definitely learn faster than before.

Socializing Your Labrador

E ven if your Lab is an only dog and you live in a rural area far away from other dogs, you should always make sure you socialize your dog. Chances are your dog is going to come into close contact with another dog at least once in its life. Your dog should also learn how to meet other people without acting badly. Properly training them how to react and act around other dogs and people can be the difference between a short, peaceful encounter and your dog acting aggressively and getting hurt. When your dog meets another person or dog, there are two things you don't want them to do. First, you don't want them to act aggressively toward it. Barking doesn't always mean aggression, but growling usually does. It may also be that the other dog may not be properly socialized, and if that's the case, you want to be able to maintain control over your dog in order to remove them from the situation and get them to safety. You also don't want them to be so scared their tail is between their legs. If your Lab is this nervous, other dogs will pick up on it as well and may perhaps get defensive or act out aggressively. You never want to be the owner of the aggressive or otherwise anti-social dog. In this section, I'll provide you with the steps you can take to do as much as you can to make sure your dog behaves healthily and is comfortable around other dogs. I'll also go through a method for socializing them as well as some extra tips.

Meeting Other Dogs

Your Lab will be most easily socialized when they're puppies, and there are different things you should do to socialize dogs at different ages, but we'll start with puppies.

Lab puppies are the easiest to socialize because everything is still new to them, meaning they're not yet completely used to being the only dog around. Like college kids, young Labs are highly open to new experiences, and they're more likely to approach things with curiosity rather than aggression. The best thing you can do to socialize your puppy with other dogs is to expose them to dogs. You should make sure the dogs you're exposing them to are safe and non-aggressive, as little as one bad experience can sour them to other dogs for the rest of their lives. Go to clubs for dog enthusiasts as these places are more likely to have experienced, dedicated dog owners whose dogs don't react negatively to other dogs. Do this often, as most dogs that are aggressive to other dogs are aggressive because they haven't been exposed to other dogs as puppies.

Socializing an adolescent Lab to be around other dogs is harder than it is to socialize a puppy, but still easier than socializing a full grown adult dog. The only way to socialize a Lab is to expose it to other dogs. Adolescent dogs are more likely to react negatively to new dogs than puppies, which is why it's important not to expose them to too many dogs too quickly. They also shouldn't immediately have dogs directly near them. A good place to socialize Labs of these ages is at the dog park. Dog parks usually have plenty of space, and surely there will be an area within it where you can play with your dog while not having other dogs too near it. While your dog probably won't act out aggressively, chances are they will be frightened. It is important that you don't punish your dog for being frightened. You should also be sure not to put them into situations they can't handle which may overwhelm them. Start slow. Bring your Lab closer and closer to other dogs while giving them time to adjust. If they begin to react negatively, move back and wait for them to calm down. Chances are they won't be completely socialized the first time. You'll have to commit to the process of socializing your dog for a few weeks.

Adult Labs are the hardest to socialize. Adult Labs that aren't used to other dogs are the most likely dogs to act aggressively when around other dogs. Since puppies and adolescent dogs must be exposed to other dogs as the only way to keep them socialized, in the same way, there's no other way to socialize an adult dog with other dogs besides than to expose it to them. Just because your adult dog isn't socialized or has reacted negatively to other dogs in the past doesn't mean it has to be deprived of the company its whole life. Adult dogs that aren't socialized must be introduced to other dogs very slowly. This means pushing them very slowly. Try just going on walks in areas where they may see other dogs from a distance. Go to dog parks weekly, keeping your distance from other dogs until you are completely sure your dog can handle going closer. You can also take it to new places at a slow pace. Try taking it to a new place once a week. You may also try to introduce it to other activities around other dogs at the same rate. It may take a while, but your dog will eventually get socialized. If you are worried about your dog acting aggressively, you should consider getting them a muzzle to wear around other dogs until you're sure they can handle it.

Meeting New People

In the same way a dog must meet other dogs to be comfortable around other dogs, your dog must meet new people to be comfortable around new people.

Puppies have the easiest time becoming socialized with other dogs as well as people. There aren't very many puppies who treat new people with hostility because they don't feel the need to be suspicious towards other people. The best thing you can do to socialize your dog towards other people is to have them meet people as often as possible. The more often your dog meets people, the easier it will be for them. There isn't much you have to do to facilitate this.

Puppies love everyone and everyone loves puppies.

When your dog gets older without gaining experience in meeting other people, however, meeting people can be intimidating for them and problematic. New people and unfamiliar faces can make older dogs nervous when they're not used to seeing new faces. There are a few things you can do to help facilitate this process and make your Lab more comfortable meeting new people. The first thing you can do is to introduce them to one person at a time. Don't try to overwhelm your Lab by bringing in a bunch of people at once. They'll freak out and act negatively. The second thing you can do is to warn the person you're introducing them so that they should come in slowly and quietly and gently. Coming in with a calm vibe can help an older dog get comfortable quicker with a new person. You should make sure the dog gets familiar with the person by smelling them and perhaps getting petted by them. But don't let the person just walk over to them. Let the dog approach the person. You should always let your Lab meet people at its own pace.

Extra Games and Commands to Teach Your Labrador

O nce you Lab has a good grasp over the basic commands and knows a few fun games to play, it can be fun and helpful for both of you to teach it new commands and games. It keeps your time together interesting and fun. Constantly learning new commands and games can help your dog stay sharp and alert. It also makes you a better owner as you come to a deeper understanding of your dog's behavior. Also, it strengthens the bond between the two of you. Teaching your dog new commands and games can also keep your dog glued to you. When a dog is challenged by something you give it, it's going to focus on you more and more to overcome it. A Lab that's constantly learning new games and commands has a much larger attention span than other dogs.

In this section, I'll give you some fun, interesting new commands, and games that you can play and do with your dog. However, before you start trying to do these things with your dog, you should make sure your dog has mastered and can consistently do all the basic commands. This ensures you can keep your dog from getting distracted as well as ensuring that they have the ability to pay close attention to your words and actions.

New Commands

The "off" command. This is a useful command if you have a Lab that likes to jump up on people to say high. It's a command that basically tells them to move away from you. You can do this command by holding a treat in your hand and keeping it closed. You get hold your hand down against your dog's nose. They'll sniff it and eventually move back once they realize that the hand is closed. As they do this, say "off." When they've moved all the way back, give them a treat. Do this over and over again until you can get them to move back with the simple command.

The "out" command. This command is meant to simply make the dog get something out of their mouth. It can be learned by playing the simple game of tug-of-war. You don't need treats to teach them this one. Get a rope or something else the two of you can play tug-of-war with and have them bite it and then try to take it away from them. Play for a while and don't let them win. Instead, keep pulling on it until you Lab lets go. As soon as it's out of their mouth, say out. Do this over and over again until they drop the toy at this simple command.

The "leave it" command. This command is the act of putting a treat or something else the dog wants in close proximity to them and instructing them to "leave it" or to not eat or touch it. You teach them to it by getting two treats and holding one in each hand. Hide one in one hand and show the dog the treat in the other. Put it right in front of their face and let them smell or lick at it. Once they realize you're not going to let go or give them the treat, they'll usually back off and might growl a little. When they do this, say "leave it." Once they're still, give them the treat in the other hand. Do this over and over again until they can obey the command without you having to wait. Once they can do this, try throwing a treat on the ground and see if they obey the command then.

The "bed" command. This command is the simple act of getting your Lab to go over to its bed. To teach them this trick, you'll need a treat and a leash. Hook them onto the leash and put a treat in your other hand. Direct your dog over to their bed (or where ever they sleep) with both the treat and the leash. Once your Lab gets there, say "bed" and give them a treat. Try this over and over again until you don't have to guide them with the leash, then try it without the treat. It should get to the point where they'll go over to their bed by the simple command. This will make it easy to get your dog in bed for the night.

The "stand up" command. This command is commanding your dog to stand on its hind legs and butt. Before you teach them this, they need to know the "sit" command. It's taught using a treat. You command the Lab to sit and then hold a treat out over their head. They'll reach for it higher and higher until they're forced to stand on their hind legs. When they do this, give them the treat and say "stand up."

The "no" command. This is an important command for your dog to know. If it's doing something it shouldn't or going somewhere it shouldn't or anything like that, this can help your dog turn its attention back to you and stop whatever might happen. To teach this, you need a leash and a treat. You place the treat on the ground, put your Lab on the leash, and slowly walk your Lab over towards it. When the treat gets your Lab's attention and it goes to eat it, pull back softly on the leash and say "no." Then give them a treat. Do this over and over again until they back away from the treat without you having to pull back. Then try it without a leash.

The "calm down" command. This is a good command for your dog to know which you can use when your dog gets overly-excited. Its purpose is to get your dog to hold still and calm down. To teach them this trick, you need a treat and a leash. Using the leash, lead your dog to a couch or other soft area. Get them to lie down in the area and then say "settle down" and give them a treat. Then direct them back up and lead them right outside the area and say "okay" and give them another treat. Do this until you don't have to guide them when you say either command.

The "heel" command. This is a good command for your dog to know when going for walks. If your Lab gets really good at it, it could even be the first step to not having to use a leash on a walk. Basically, it's just the command that tells your dog it's supposed to be walking or standing right to the side of your legs, its front legs parallel with yours. You'll need a leash and a treat. You can tie the leash into your belt loop, making your dog unable to walk anywhere other than beside you but not too tight it's uncomfortable for them. Then try walking with them. Every time your Lab pulls on the leash, go in the opposite direction as they are pulling. When the leash becomes loose, say "heel" and give them a treat. Do this over and over again until they can "heel" at command. Then try it without a leash.

New Games

Exotic fetching. Throwing the same ball every time you play fetch with your dog can get a little boring. Keep yourself and your Lab interested in the game by getting some different things to play fetch with. Try stuffed animals or other types of toys. You can also try throwing things that might be a little difficult for your dog to pick up and bring back to you.

Frisbee. Frisbee is one of the most beloved dog games. To play this game, your dog should already know how to fetch. What's good about Frisbee in the fact that the object doesn't fall right to the ground. Instead, it hovers in the air and moves much slower than a regular ball. If your dog's fast enough, which they probably are, they can run and catch up to it. If you do this enough and your dog gets really good, they can even catch it in the air. Not only is this game fun, as you get to throw a Frisbee, you also get the immense pleasure of watching your dog catch a Frisbee in the air. It's also very impressive to strangers.

Fight the Water. You've probably seen videos online of dogs going crazy trying to bite the stream of water shooting out of hoses. Well, if you didn't know, Labs love water. All you need to play this game is a yard, a hose, and a water source. Simply point the house slightly up into the air, maybe spraying your dog at first to get their attention. Soon they'll be jumping up at it and going crazy. A big benefit of this game is that, while it makes your dog go crazy and expend a bunch of energy, all you have to do is hold the hose. So this is a good game for you to play with your dog when it's just one of those days where you're just too tired to do much else.

The Chase. Dogs are predators. Few things can get dogs as excited as chasing a squirrel or other wild animal. Well, this is a way to play into that part of your Lab without anything having to die. How you play this game is by getting a stuffed animal and tying it to a long rope. Get your Lab interested in it and then pull it away from them as fast as you can. They'll run after it and try to catch it. When it gets back to you, throw it out and repeat the process.

Soccer. A fun game to play with your dog is to get a soccer ball, which is probably a bigger object than your dog can fit in its mouth, and kick it around. They'll run after the ball and go crazy. You can just keep kicking it and watch them chase after it. They'll try to bite is and it'll just get further away from them. Very funny to watch!

Flirt Pole. A Flirt Pole is a long stick with a lure at the end of it. You tease your dog with the lure and then watch as it chases it around. It's a really good game when you don't feel like doing much because all you have to do is move the stick and watch the dog wear itself out. When you're playing this, make sure to tone it down from time to time. This can really tire dogs out as they make sharp turns and sprint to catch the lure. You should also be sure to let your dog catch the lure every once in a while to keep their interest.

Bubbles. This is another game where you don't have to do much. All you need is some soapy water and a bubble blower. Get your Lab near you and blow some bubbles. Now watch as it goes crazy trying to get them. Just keep blowing bubbles around them and they'll entertain themselves. It's also fun to watch the bubbles pop on your Lab's nose!

Find the Treat. The last game we'll cover is a simple game of hiding one of your dog's favorite treats. Have them sit in another room or on the other side of a big room. Then hide the treat on the floor or on a short counter. Then release them from their place and watch as they look furiously for the treat. You can play this on days when you can go outside and it doesn't require much exercise on your part.

Conclusion

There's a reason Labrador Retrievers are the most popular dogs in the United States. They are smart dogs that get along well with both children and other dogs. A Labrador Retriever brings people together and completes a family because they are part of the family. For thousands of years, dogs and humans have shared the same living spaces and enjoyed each other's company. Having a dog in your life can be the difference between a home that is empty, quiet, and lonely to a home that is vibrant, warm, and loving. Dogs serve as a faithful companion that is always loving and accepting, no matter who you are or what you do.

However, there is a difference between having a Labrador Retriever that's not trained and having a Labrador Retriever that's well trained. Having a well-trained Labrador Retriever opens up your options. You can go more places, meet more dogs, and meet more people. You can take them to huge parks in the country and let them run around off their leash without having to worry about them running away and getting into trouble because they'll always come back to you and they'll always respond to your commands. Being well-trained is also a huge benefit to the Labrador itself. They get challenges. They feel as though they have a purpose. They have little jobs to do, and dogs love having jobs to do. Well-trained Labs also have an incredibly fulfilling relationship with their owners. The bond an owner gets with their dog in the process of training is one of the closest bonds any one person can have with a dog. A well-trained dog can also go anywhere dogs can go. The owner never has to worry about their well-trained Lab because that Lab understands the world and the importance of order in ways that other, non-trained dogs simply don't.

It's also very beneficial to the dog owner to have a well-trained dog. It opens up your options as to where you can go with your dog and what you can do. It makes sure that the time you spend with your dog will never be boring and you won't ever feel like your dog isn't getting enough attention and you'll never be afraid that they aren't happy. It's also really good if you have children. Having a well-trained Lab is a very good thing to have around children because it will teach them how to not be afraid of dogs as well as how to treat them and raise a healthy, well-trained dog.

It's also a load of fun to train your Lab. While simply playing with your dog might get old after a while, the process of teaching a dog all the commands you can is very different. You put in the time and you never feel as if you're wasting it. At the end of every day during the training process, you see a change in your dog. It listens to you a little better. It looks at you for more cues than before. It can read your mood better. It trusts you more and is more comfortable around you. You also get to see them doing things they couldn't do before. You get to watch your Lab grow like a child. They learn new skills. They get better, faster, and stronger. You get to impress people with how well your dog is trained and you come across as a put-together, orderly person.

You also won't ever have to worry about your dog when people come over or when the two of you go somewhere. You can take it to the dog park and be relaxed and open the whole time. You don't have to worry about waking up to messes. You don't have to worry about your dog getting off its leash somehow and not being able to get a hold of it. You don't have to worry that your dog will bark all night and annoy the neighbors.

Training your dog can improve every part of its life. Well-trained dogs are far less likely to be given up for adoption than dogs that aren't trained. They're far less likely to be put down or attacked by other dogs. You don't need to fear that your dog will attack a child or kill another dog. Your dog will be calm and passive and under control as long as you're there to give it a command.

We've covered a lot of topics in this book. I hope that you found it helpful and that you learned a lot. I hope your training goes well, and please remember that it never hurts to come back to this to refresh your knowledge, or to solve problems that may arise.

About The Author

Kimberly Lawrence is a lifelong animal lover, artist and writer. Her entire career centers around animals, mainly dogs. She has owned Labs, collies, shelties, mixed breeds, and dachshunds, while fostering dozens of different breeds for rescue organizations over the years. She worked several years as a dog trainer, doing private training and classes at a board-and-train facility in San Francisco. Since then, She has been pet sitting and boarding dogs in her home for over 10 years.

Kimberly now live in Southern California with a Lab, a dachshund and two rescued cats. When not writing or walking with her dogs, Kimberly enjoys spending time horseback riding with her daughters or relaxing at the lake with her husband. She always has an assortment of guest dogs to keep her busy!